THE ARIMATHEAN ASSIGNMENT

WHY GOD ENTRUSTS WEALTH TO PROTECT WHAT IS MOST SACRED

DR. JOHN THURBER

The Arimathean Assignment: Why God Entrusts Wealth to Protect What Is Most Sacred

Paperback ISBN: 979-8-9918542-4-5
eBook ISBN: 979-8-9918542-5-2

Original Cover by Salma Designs.

Page graphics (background and ornamental break) generated using AI technology via DALL·E by OpenAI customized based on user-provided prompts and specifications. Copyright © February 19, 2026 by Lonzine Lee, Dominion Unlimited Publications. All rights reserved.

Edits and formatting by Dominion Unlimited Editorial Services, domunltd@gmail.com.

CONTENTS

To the courageous entrepreneurs who seek to navigate amidst the relentless currents of commerce by a higher compass. May your ventures not merely be engines of profit, but vessels of purpose, echoing the ancient call to steward God's creation with integrity, wisdom, and a steadfast devotion to His enduring Kingdom.

May this work serve as a guiding light, leading you toward a meaningful legacy that is not solely built on acquisition, but the richly profound, sacrificial act of safeguarding all that is precious in His sight.

FOREWORD

I am honored to write the foreword for my friend, Dr. John Thurber. I'm excited because this is a fantastic piece of writing. There are certain books that challenge your thinking. Then there are books that challenge your life. *The Arimathean Assignment* does both.

For years, many of us in business and leadership circles have looked to Joseph, son of Jacob, as the ultimate biblical model for entrepreneurship--and rightly so. His wisdom, strategy, resilience, and ability to steward resources during crisis remain extraordinary examples for leaders today. But Dr. John Thurber dares to ask a deeper question: What if Kingdom wealth was never primarily about accumulation, but about protection? That question stopped me in my tracks.

Because when you study Scripture carefully, Joseph of Arimathea emerges as something profoundly different. He was not remembered for building an empire, managing grain supply chains, or accumulating influence for its own sake. He was remembered because, in one of history's darkest moments, he used his wealth, position, courage, and reputation to protect what was most sacred to God.

He stepped forward when others stepped back. He leveraged influence when silence would have been safer. He surrendered something valuable for a Kingdom purpose that looked hopeless in the natural. That is a message this generation desperately needs.

We live in a culture that celebrates platform, visibility, scale, and personal success. Even within Christian leadership, it is easy to drift toward a version of prosperity that subtly becomes centered on ourselves—our comfort, our image, our accomplishments, and our expansion. But this book calls us back to a far more sacred understanding of stewardship.

Dr. Thurber reminds us that wealth is not simply a blessing to enjoy. It is a responsibility to deploy. Kingdom entrepreneurs are not merely called to build profitable enterprises. We are called to become protectors of what Heaven values most. We are called to safeguard truth, dignity, people, mission, integrity, and the advancing work of Christ in the earth. That perspective changes everything.

As the CEO of a regional community bank, I spend much of my life around conversations involving growth, capital, strategy, leadership, and financial stewardship. I deeply believe business can be a calling from God. I believe entrepreneurs can be some of the most influential ministers in the marketplace today. But I also believe one of the greatest dangers successful people face is slowly confusing wealth with purpose. This book confronts that danger with wisdom, boldness, and biblical depth.

What I especially appreciate about Dr. Thurber's writing is that he refuses to create a false divide between faith and enterprise. He understands that business itself can become an act of worship when it is surrendered fully to God's purposes. He presents a vision where leadership is not about self-glorification, but servant-hearted stewardship; a vision where influence is not used to elevate ourselves, but to strengthen others; a vision where success is ultimately measured not just by profitability, but by eternal impact.

The world does not merely need more wealthy Christians. It needs courageous stewards. It needs leaders who know how to respond when truth is vulnerable, when people are hurting, when integrity is costly, and when the mission of God requires sacrifice instead of applause.

It needs modern-day Josephs of Arimathea.

My prayer is that this book will deeply challenge pastors, entrepreneurs, executives, investors, nonprofit leaders, and marketplace ministers alike. I pray it awakens something eternal inside those who have succeeded financially but know there must be a greater purpose attached to their success.

Because there is.

May we all have the courage to accept the assignment.

Sean Kouplen
Chairman & CEO, Regent Bank
Cofounder, 94X Faith at Work Movement

ENDORSEMENT BY DR. BRENT THURBER

The Arimathean Assignment offers a unique and spiritually challenging perspective on wealth, leadership, and Christian entrepreneurship. Throughout the opening chapters, John contrasts the lives of Joseph, son of Jacob, and Joseph of Arimathea to redefine what true Kingdom success looks like. While Joseph of Egypt is praised for his wisdom, planning, and economic leadership, John argues that Joseph of Arimathea represents a higher calling—using wealth and influence to protect what is most sacred to God. This central idea gives the book a fresh and thought-provoking message that goes beyond traditional teachings about prosperity.

One of the book's greatest strengths is the way it combines biblical interpretation with practical lessons for today's leaders and entrepreneurs. John explains that wealth should not simply be accumulated for personal success, but should be stewarded for God's purposes. The chapters discussing stewardship, servant leadership, and God as the "ultimate CEO" challenge readers to rethink how businesses should operate. Instead of focusing only on profit, the author encourages Christians to value integrity, justice, compassion, and responsibility toward others. His emphasis on protecting the vulnerable and advancing God's Kingdom gives the book both spiritual depth and real-world application.

The comparison between the two Josephs is especially compelling. Joseph, son of Jacob, demonstrates wisdom in managing resources and preserving nations during famine, while Joseph of Arimathea demonstrates courage and sacrificial stewardship by caring for Jesus' body during a moment of vulnerability. My brother uses this contrast to show that Kingdom wealth is not merely about gaining influence, but about using influence faithfully and courageously.

The chapter "Beyond the Golden Calf" also provides a strong warning against turning wealth into an idol, reminding readers that money should remain a tool for service rather than an object of worship. Is money your master—or your servant? Money highlights what is in an individual's heart.

Overall, *The Arimathean Assignment* is an inspiring and insightful book for Christians, business leaders, and anyone interested in faith-based leadership. John successfully blends theology, ethics, and entrepreneurship into a message that is both challenging and encouraging. His writing encourages readers to move beyond self-centered ambition and embrace a model of stewardship rooted in sacrifice, integrity, and eternal purpose. The book leaves a lasting impression by reminding readers that true Kingdom success is measured not by what we possess, but by how faithfully we use what God has entrusted to us.

Dr. Brent Thurber

Lead Pastor

The Stronghold

SPECIAL THANKS

I wish to express my profound gratitude to the many individuals whose insights, encouragement, and unwavering support have been instrumental in bringing this work to fruition. My sincere thanks go to the mentors who first illuminated the intersection of theology and commerce, whose wisdom continues to guide my own entrepreneurial journey.

I am indebted to the leaders and innovators within the Kingdom-business movement whose lives and ministries serve as living parables, demonstrating the practical outworking of biblical principles in the marketplace.

My family deserves special recognition for their patience, understanding, and for being a constant source of inspiration and grounding.

Finally, I offer my deepest thanks to the Almighty, the ultimate source of all wisdom and enterprise, whose grace has made this endeavor possible.

INTRODUCTION

This book undertakes a re-examination of Kingdom entrepreneurship, proposing a paradigm shift from the prosperity-focused narrative of Joseph, son of Jacob, to the sacrificial stewardship embodied by Joseph of Arimathea. While Jacob's son masterfully managed resources to avert famine and preserve life, demonstrating remarkable acumen and divine favor, I contend that the ultimate measure of Kingdom wealth does not lie solely in acquisition but in the capacity to protect and safeguard what is most precious to God. This profound responsibility extends to His people, His mission, and the very integrity of His unfolding purposes in the world.

Joseph of Arimathea, a figure often relegated to a footnote in the grand sweep of salvation history, emerges in these pages as a compelling exemplar of this higher calling. A businessman of considerable means, he leveraged his influence and resources not for personal gain, but for an act of profound theological significance. He ensured the dignified burial of Jesus, thereby safeguarding the nascent Christian movement during its most vulnerable hour. Joseph's actions underscore a principle far removed from mere wealth creation; they speak to a spirit of courageous, timely stewardship—a "Christ protection" model that contrasts sharply with the "wealth creation" narrative.

Through an in-depth analysis of biblical narratives and contemporary business ethics, this work is an exploration of foundational Kingdom principles. We will examine the concept of God as the ultimate CEO, the transformative power of servant-hearted leadership, the non-negotiable imperative of radical integrity, and the Quadruple Bottom Line: People, Planet, Profitability, and Eternity, understood through a distinctly divine lens.

The aim is to equip modern business leaders with practical insights and prayer points, challenging them to embrace a first-responder stewardship mentality. This calls for positioning their enterprises not just for market success, but as vital instruments for safeguarding and advancing God's purposes on earth, fulfilling a divine mandate for generosity and enduring impact.

ONE
GOD'S STANDARD FOR KINGDOM ENTREPRENEURS

I have been using the term **"Kingdompreneur"** within the business ministry at my church, The Stronghold[1] for quite a while; however, a new dimension was added to my study through an online teaching. After hearing a brief message on Joseph of Arimathea by Apostle Dr. Francis Myles, my spirit was stirred so deeply to pursue this line of study that I want to begin by sharing the following quotes and thoughts gleaned from that same message. They represent what I consider to be key turning points and revelations that shaped this book.

In his teaching, Dr. Myles declared:

> *Joseph of Arimathea is God's standard for Kingdom Entrepreneurship.*[2]

> The Lord said, *"You love to use Joseph, son of Jacob, as your God standard on Kingdom entrepreneurship. ...Use a*

---

1. The Stronghold Church, Sand Springs, Oklahoma.
2. Francis Myles, "The 'Other Joseph' God Showed Me About Kingdom Entrepreneurship w/ Taylor Welch," *YouTube* video, 37:13, posted December 9, 2025, https://youtu.be/XAqid_sT6Sw, at 18:25.

better model. Joseph, son of Jacob, was the beginning of Me weaving the mantle of Kingdom entrepreneurship—not the end of the matter."

God identifies the overlooked model: "My God-standard Kingdom entrepreneurship lies in the hands of another Joseph... Joseph of Arimathea."

Warning: *"If you stay with Joseph, son of Jacob, you are going to produce the kind of businesspeople who can become wealthy, but can't protect Me."*

The Lord highlights His most priceless piece of real estate on earth—His incorruptible body—and the moment He was most vulnerable... dead on the Cross.

He asks, *"Who did I use to rescue that lifeless, vulnerable body? A businessman by the name of Joseph of Arimathea."*

Core insight: *"The reason for wealth is to rescue My body when it's most vulnerable."*

Holy-Spirit Highlights

These are the spiritual insights and emotional highlights I experienced and expressed aloud after hearing this message.

1. Awe at discovering a fuller, protective purpose for Kingdom wealth.

2. A shift from admiration of the prosperity message (Joseph, son of Jacob) alone to a call for sacrificial stewardship (Joseph of Arimathea) which fully encompasses the Kingdom wealth message.
3. God redirects entrepreneurial role models from wealth acquisition to Christ protection.
4. True Kingdom prosperity positions believers to safeguard what is most sacred to God.
5. Kingdom businesspeople are called to be first responders when Christ's body—His people, His mission—is at risk.

As I prayed to understand how to incorporate these points into my life and teaching, these two prayer points and next steps were given to me by the Holy Spirit.

1. Pray for business leaders to embrace Joseph of Arimathea's mantle: courageous, timely stewardship that protects the Body of Christ.
2. Ask the Lord to reveal practical ways wealth can "rescue" vulnerable parts of His Church today.

With those instructions in mind, we will commence with a closer examination of the two Josephs' respective resumes, beginning with the son of Jacob.

TWO
JOSEPH, SON OF JACOB
AN ENTREPRENEURIAL RESUME

Students of the Old Testament are well aware that Joseph, son of Jacob, demonstrated remarkable entrepreneurial traits during his time in Egypt. His leadership skills were noted first as a slave in the household of Potiphar,[1] second during his prison years,[2] and finally in the palace of the Egyptian king,[3] where his strategic foresight, risk management, and leadership are still studied today.

By correctly interpreting Pharaoh's dream[4] to foresee a famine, Joseph was then positioned to mastermind Egypt's grain storage and distribution,[5] effectively becoming, in modern terms, a CEO managing a national supply chain and improving Egypt's economy. By divine appointment, he turned a potential disaster into prosperity through astute planning and stewardship, making him a biblical figure

1. Genesis 39:1-6 (NKJV).
2. Genesis 39:21-23 (NKJV).
3. Genesis 41:39-44 (NKJV).
4. Genesis 41:1-36 (NKJV).
5. Genesis 41:33-36, 48-49 (NKJV).

praised for his business acumen and ability to create value from adversity.

Joseph's Entrepreneurial Journey (Genesis 37–50)[6]

1. **Early Signs of Favor and Vision:** As Jacob's favored son, Joseph received a coat of many colors (symbolizing status) and had prophetic dreams (family bowing to him) that fueled jealousy but also foreshadowed his future leadership.
2. **From Slavery to Steward:** Sold into slavery by his brothers, Joseph thrived in Potiphar's house, showing integrity and capability, managing all aspects of the household, a precursor to large-scale management.
3. **Prison to Power Broker:** Even in prison, Joseph's ability to interpret the dreams of fellow prisoners led to his interpreting Pharaoh's dream of seven fat years followed by seven lean years, revealing God's plan.
4. **Strategic Planning & Execution:** Joseph advised Pharaoh to store surplus grain during the abundance, essentially creating a national strategic reserve—a massive logistics and inventory management project.
5. **National Leadership & Wealth Creation:** During the famine, Joseph controlled Egypt's resources, selling grain not just for money but also for land and

---

6. The narrative of Joseph, son of Jacob's life and leadership appears in Genesis 37–50 (NKJV).

loyalty, which consolidated Pharaoh's economic power, increasing his centralized wealth and empire. (Genesis 47:20-26).

6. **Supply Chain Management:** He organized grain storage throughout the cities and oversaw distribution during the famine, balancing supply and demand for fourteen years, demonstrating sophisticated strategies comparable to our modern-day warehouses, distribution centers, inventory systems, and supply chain and operations management. (Genesis 41:48-49, 6; 47:14).

Key Entrepreneurial Qualities

Vision & Foresight: Saw beyond immediate circumstances to long-term needs (famine).

Resilience & Adaptability: Turned slavery and imprisonment into opportunities for growth.

Stewardship & Integrity: Managed resources responsibly, building trust.

Strategic Thinking: Developed complex plans (grain storage) for national benefit.

Leadership: Rose from prisoner to second-in-command, guiding a nation.

SUMMARY

Joseph, son of Jacob's resume illustrates how faith, vision, and strategic execution can build immense value and save a nation, making him a noteworthy example for business and leadership students.

THREE
JOSEPH OF ARIMATHEA
AN ENTREPRENEURIAL RESUME

Unlike Joseph, son of Jacob, whose life is narrated extensively across thirteen chapters in the book of Genesis, Joseph of Arimathea appears in the biblical text only in connection with the burial of Jesus (Matthew 27:57–60; Mark 15:43–46; Luke 23:50–53; John 19:38–42). But within that short record we find a portrait of wealth, influence, courage, and decisive stewardship at the most critical moment of humanity's redemptive history.

Arimathea, as described in Luke 23:51, was situated in the hill country region of Judea, likely within the Shephelah area. Numerous scholars identify it with the Old Testament Ramathaim-Zophim, later shortened to Ramah, traditionally linked to the prophet Samuel (1 Samuel 1:1). The town is also mentioned in 1 Maccabees 11:34 and in Josephus's *Antiquities of the Jews (*13.4.9), solidifying its recognition as a Judean locality during the Second Temple period. Early Christian writers like Eusebius and Jerome also associated Arimathea with Ramah. Although its exact location remains a subject of debate, historical records confirm that Joseph of Arimathea hailed from a genuine and identifiable Jewish town—not a mythical construct.[1]

From the four Gospels we see a portrait of Joseph as a "man of Arimathea, a city of the Jews." He is painted as a prominent council member, secret disciple of Jesus, and as a rich and respected Jew who demonstrated a faith-driven act of Kingdom entrepreneurship by providing his own tomb for Jesus' burial (cf. Matthew 27:60).

Beyond the biblical accounts, tradition and legend expand Joseph's story in ways that have shaped Christian imagination through the centuries. Medieval and post-medieval sources associate Joseph with trade and early Christian enterprise, though these accounts are not part of the canonical witness.

For example, some British and devotional traditions portray Joseph as a prosperous merchant engaged in the tin trade between the Near East and Cornwall, one who is sometimes credited with influence among Roman authorities. In these accounts, his position and resources are said to be what enabled him to minister to the early Christian movement and to act decisively after the crucifixion.

One legendary narrative found on Mazed Tales[2] portrays Joseph of Arimathea traveling widely as a merchant, possibly

---

1. See Jerry A. Pattengale, "Arimathea (Place)," in *The Anchor Bible Dictionary*, vol. 1, ed. David Noel Freedman (New York: Doubleday, 1992), 378; and standard reference works such as *The International Standard Bible Encyclopedia*, s.v. "Arimathea."
2. *Mazed Tales*, "Joseph of Arimathea," a modern retelling of British and

bringing the young boy Jesus (described as his great-nephew) with him on trading voyages, explained as being part of Jesus' lost years. Joseph is then later credited with establishing early Christian presence in Britain.

Such narratives also connect Joseph with building Britain's first church at Glastonbury, where he supposedly planted his staff, which grew into what became the Glastonbury Thorn.[3] A later legendary tale associates him with bringing the *Holy Grail* (the cup from the Last Supper) to England, then hiding it at the Chalice Well in Glastonbury.[4]

All of these type of stories link Joseph's material wealth to sacred relics, but they belong more to the realm of folklore than to verifiable history. What is noteworthy is how these legendary images have contributed to make the person of Joseph of Arimathea an interesting study of lasting cultural and devotional significance, illustrating how he has been interpreted through the lenses of scripture, business, and myth.

Arthurian Christian legend, accessed February 18, 2026, https://www.mazedtales.org/tales/joseph-arimathea.

3. William of Malmesbury, *De Antiquitate Glastoniensis Ecclesiae* (On the Antiquity of the Church of Glastonbury), 12th century.

4. Glastonbury Quest for the Holy Grail," *National Catholic Register* (EWTN), May 28, 2021, accessed February 18, 2026, https://www.ncregister.com/features/joseph-of-arimathea-and-the-glastonbury-quest-for-the-holy-grail; cf. Mazed Tales, "Joseph of Arimathea," a modern retelling of British and Arthurian Christian legend, accessed February 18, 2026, https://www.mazedtales.org/tales/joseph-arimathea.ncregister+2

AS A MODEL OF FAITH-DRIVEN BUSINESS, JOSEPH OF Arimathea demonstrates the wisdom available to acquire and use wealth within God's Kingdom, exercising the vision to prioritize and protect what is most sacred to God. His story inspires modern interpretations of using business acumen for spiritual purposes, focusing on sacrifice, integrity, and building God's Kingdom.

Early Christian Business: He's seen as a "Kingdom entrepreneur" for using his wealth and position to support his faith, offering his own tomb for Jesus and later, in legend, establishing churches and bringing Christian artifacts to Britain.

Kingdom Alignment: Waited for the Kingdom of God—and acted in alignment with it.

Influence with Courage: Used his access to power at a moment of maximum vulnerability.

Roman Connections: His social standing granted him access to Roman leaders, including Pontius Pilate, enabling him to request Jesus' body after the crucifixion.

Stewardship Under Risk: Placed reputation and resources on the line when Christ's body required protection.

Wealth With Restraint: He possessed means but did not flaunt them.

COMPARISON/CONTRAST: LEGACY OF TWO RESUMES

Legendary Entrepreneurship & Influence: Joseph, son of Jacob's entrepreneurial skill resulted in accumulation and centralized economic power, while Joseph of Arimathea's defining act involved relinquishment of personal safety and anonymity to protect what mattered most to God—the body of Christ.

Limited and Eternal Acts of Preservation: Joseph, son of Jacob preserved a nation through accumulation and strategy, while Joseph of Arimathea preserved the Messiah's body, God's most valued treasure, through sacrifice and courage.

Wealth Optimization, National, Global, and Kingdom Influence: Joseph, son of Jacob, demonstrates how God's wisdom empowers us to create wealth that builds systems and provides long-term national solutions regardless of circumstantial or economic hardship, while Joseph of Arimathea demonstrates the necessity of clearly operating in God's wisdom and understanding to be able to steward what He values most and influence global communities through His Kingdom.

ETERNAL IMPACT OF NECESSITY TO EFFECTIVELY USE WEALTH

Joseph, son of Jacob demonstrates how God's wisdom helps us to optimize wealth's capacity to build systems and provide long-term solutions even in the midst of circumstantial or economic hardship.

Joseph of Arimathea demonstrates the wisdom we have available to acquire and use wealth within God's Kingdom, exercising the vision to prioritize and protect what is most sacred to God.

FOUR
BEYOND THE GOLDEN CALF
RE-EVALUATING KINGDOM WEALTH

In the story of Joseph, son of Jacob, we see a powerful paradigm of astute resource management and divine enablement that led to immense accumulation and the preservation of life. As we delve deeper into the true nature of Kingdom wealth, we must prepare to confront a question of significant spiritual peril: what happens when the seductive whisper of wealth, amplified by the engine of commerce, morphs into a deafening roar that drowns out the subtler promptings of divine purpose?

As Christian entrepreneurs, we face a significant temptation, the insidious transformation of a divinely provided tool into an object of worship. This spiritual deception leads to an unseen cost—the hidden price required when we choose wealth over God as our ultimate reward for ambition and devotion. We see an example of this when we look at the exodus of the ancient Israelites. Powerfully delivered from the bondage of Egypt, they stood at the precipice of a profound spiritual covenant.

Yet, within months of witnessing the awe-inspiring power of God at the Red Sea, they succumbed to a primal act of idolatry while Moses, their divinely appointed leader, was meeting with God on Mount Sinai, receiving the very law that would govern their relationship with Him and each other.[1] In his delayed absence, the people demanded that Aaron craft a tangible representation of the divine, a visible object of godlike presence and power. They said to Aaron,

> "Come, make us gods that shall go before us; for *as for* this Moses, the man who brought us up out of the land of Egypt, we do not know what has become of him."
>
> EXODUS 32:1

It's a well-documented truth that when divine outcomes differ from mankind's expectations, even those who have experienced profound divine intervention can fall prey to fallacy. By placing their trust and ultimate allegiance in human effort and material possessions, the Israelites did not receive a true reflection of their Deliverer, the transcendent, covenant-making God.

> And he received *the gold* from their hand, and he fashioned it with an engraving tool, and made a molded calf. Then they said, "This *is* your god, O Israel, that brought you out of the land of Egypt!"
>
> EXODUS 32:4

1. Exodus 14; Exodus 19:1-8; Exodus 24:12-18; Exodus 31:18-32:1-8 (NKJV).

Aaron fashioned a golden calf. This crude idol, the return on their own investments of material wealth, symbolized their desire for immediate, palpable security and power. However, it is their words and Aaron's actions, condemned by God Himself, that made their sin so great, and serve as a timeless cautionary tale.

> So when Aaron saw *it*, he built an altar before it. And Aaron made a proclamation and said, "Tomorrow *is* a feast to the LORD."
>
> EXODUS 32:5

THE PARALLELS BETWEEN THE ISRAELITES' WORSHIP OF THE golden calf and the modern Kingdom entrepreneur's potentially idolatrous pursuit of wealth are striking. Entrepreneurs, often driven by a desire to create, build, and provide, can find their focus increasingly fixed on the metrics of financial success. Profit margins, market share, and revenue growth become the tangible manifestations of their efforts—the visible signs of their self-powered "prosperity," something God specifically warned the Israelites to look out for.[2]

2. Deuteronomy 8:11-20.

While such metrics are not inherently evil, they can, if left unchecked, eclipse the spiritual realities they are meant to serve. When wealth becomes an end in itself, the pursuit fosters a self-referential system where success is measured solely by accumulation, and ultimate authority subtly shifts from the God who grants the ability to create wealth to the wealth itself.

For eons, humanity has been captivated by the many forms of wealth pursuit. We are drawn to its promise of security, comfort, and influence. In the realm of business, this allure is amplified. The drive to acquire, to grow, and to accumulate can be a powerful engine of innovation and productivity. Yet, within the framework of faith and enterprise, this relentless pursuit can also become a treacherous path, leading us away from the very principles we seek to uphold.

As we move beyond the seductive allure of mere accumulation, a more robust and biblically resonant paradigm for Kingdom wealth begins to emerge. This paradigm is not defined by what we gather, but by what we are empowered to protect and to advance. It shifts the entrepreneurial focus from personal prosperity and the satisfaction of individual ambition to a divinely ordained mandate for safeguarding and nurturing that which is most precious to the heart of God: His people and His ongoing mission in the world.

This is the essence of stewardship, not as a passive management of resources, but as an active, often sacrificial, commitment to ensuring the well-being and the continued progress of the Kingdom. It requires a redefinition of success, moving from a metric of personal net worth to a measure of our capacity for selfless responsibility and altruism. This reorientation lays the essential groundwork for understanding the profound significance of individuals like Joseph of Arimathea, who embodied this higher calling, demonstrating that true Kingdom wealth finds its ultimate expression not in hoarding, but in courageous and timely action for the sake of God's enduring purposes.

THE WEIGHT OF LEADERSHIP IN ANY ENTERPRISE, WHETHER IT'S a burgeoning startup or a multinational corporation, can feel immense. We grapple with market fluctuations, competitor strategies, employee well-being, and the relentless pressure to innovate and grow. In this complex dance of strategy and execution, it is easy for the human leader to assume a position of ultimate control, becoming the sole architect and arbiter of his or her venture's destiny. Yet, a deeper theological lens reveals a profound truth that radically reorients our understanding of leadership and success: God is the ultimate CEO. This is not a mere metaphorical flourish; it is a foundational theological assertion that redefines our role from master of our domain to faithful steward of a divinely orchestrated reality.

This perspective draws its origin from the very beginning of creation. The Genesis account does not present a distant, uninvolved deity who set the universe in motion and then retreated. Instead, it depicts a God who is actively involved, shaping, ordering, and breathing life into existence. In Genesis 1, we witness God speaking, bringing forth light, separating waters, and populating the earth with life. These are not the movements of a passive CEO delegating every task to a management team from the outset. It is sovereign action, direct and intentional. God is the prime mover, the source of all being, and the ultimate authority over all that has been created. Every resource, every opportunity, every innovation ultimately originates from this divine wellspring.[3]

When we establish an enterprise, we are not creating something *ex nihilo*; we are entering into a pre-existing reality that is fundamentally governed by God's sovereignty. The very laws of physics, principles of economics, and the capacity for human ingenuity are all gifts and instruments of this overarching divine governance.

This understanding of God as the ultimate CEO extends beyond the initial act of creation into His ongoing covenantal relationship with humanity. Throughout the Old Testament, we see Him establishing covenants—promises and agreements that shape the trajectory of His people and their interactions with the world. These covenants are not mere diplomatic pacts; they are declarations of God's active partnership and guiding hand in human affairs.

---

3. James 1:17; 1 Chronicles 29:11-12 (NKJV).

When God made a covenant with Abraham, promising to make him a great nation and bless him, He was not simply offering a vague assurance. He was establishing a framework for Abraham's life and endeavors, a divine endorsement and direction for his stewardship. Similarly, the Mosaic covenant established a way of life, a set of principles for governance, justice, and economic activity that was intended to reflect God's character and purposes. These covenants underscore a crucial point: God is not an absentee landlord. He is intimately involved in the details of His creation and the enterprises undertaken within it; therefore, when we step into leadership roles within our businesses, we are stepping onto a stage where God is already the senior partner, the ultimate authority.

Our position is not one of absolute dominion, but of delegated responsibility. We are stewards, entrusted with managing the resources, talents, and opportunities that God has placed within our sphere of influence.

This shifts the locus of control dramatically. Instead of seeing ourselves as the sole originators of success, we recognize that our achievements are, in part, a manifestation of God's grace and His provision. This fosters a profound sense of humility. The arrogance that can easily accompany entrepreneurial success is tempered by the understanding that we are not ultimately in charge. Our strategies, our insights, our hard work are all valuable, but they operate within a divinely established order and are ultimately subject to His purposes.

This perspective compels a deeper reliance on God's wisdom. In the Genesis account, the early humans were given dominion over creation, but this was not a mandate for unchecked exploitation.[4] It was a call to responsible stewardship, a task that would undoubtedly require discernment and understanding, qualities that are best sought from the Creator Himself. Proverbs is replete with admonishments to seek wisdom from God, to incline our hearts to understanding, and to acknowledge Him in all our ways.

For the entrepreneur, this translates into prayerful deliberation before making critical decisions, seeking divine guidance in strategic planning, and a willingness to pivot when our human-devised plans conflict with what we discern to be God's leading. It means not relying solely on market analysis or competitor intelligence, but integrating a spiritual dimension into our decision-making processes. This paradigm is not about abandoning sound business principles, but about imbuing them with a divine perspective, seeking to align our commercial pursuits with God's eternal objectives.

The ultimate measure of success, therefore, is not solely determined by profit margins, market share, or exit valuations. Metrics such as these are important indicators of operational effectiveness within the earthly realm, but are insufficient as the ultimate arbiter of a venture's true success from a Kingdom perspective. The Bible consistently emphasizes faithfulness, integrity, and the advancement of God's purposes as the hallmarks of true achievement. When we view ourselves as stewards under God, success is redefined as

---

4. Genesis 1:26-28; Psalm 8:4-8 (NKJV).

fulfilling the responsibilities He has assigned us, using the resources He has provided in a manner that honors Him and benefits His creation.

This could involve making a challenging ethical choice that temporarily affects profitability but aligns with Kingdom values. It might entail investing in employee development and well-being even when it doesn't immediately enhance the bottom line. It might even mean prioritizing long-term, sustainable growth that respects environmental stewardship over short-term, exploitative gains.

FIVE
THE KINGDOM STEWARDSHIP MODEL

The narrative of creation in Genesis 1, with its repeated refrain of "and God saw that it was good," highlights a divine affirmation of creative work. God Himself is the worker, and He declares His handiwork to be good. This implies that business, when conducted according to divine principles, is not a secular activity separate from God's purposes, but an arena where His work can and should be done. This understanding transforms the entrepreneur's role from a mere capitalist seeking personal gain to a participant in God's ongoing redemptive project.

Consider the implications of this for leadership styles. Enterprises can become extensions of God's creative and redemptive mission in the world. They can be platforms for demonstrating integrity, fostering community, providing goods and services that genuinely serve human needs, and generating resources that can be stewarded for the advancement of the Kingdom.

If God is the ultimate CEO, then the human leader is a vice-president, a general manager, or a project lead, always accountable to a higher authority. This promotes a servant-leadership model, mirroring Christ's own example and discouraging the autocratic tendencies that can plague leadership. This is a principle Jesus taught His disciples.

> "But it is not this way among you. Instead whoever wants to become great among you must be your servant, and whoever wants to be first among you must be the slave of all. For even the Son of Man did not come to be served, but to serve, and to give his life as a ransom for many."
>
> MARK 10:43-45 NET

This radical reorientation of power and authority is directly applicable to the business world. Leaders who understand God as the ultimate CEO seek to empower their teams, fostering an environment of mutual respect and collaboration. They prioritize the well-being and growth of their employees, recognizing them as individuals created in God's image, rather than mere cogs in a profit-generating machine.

Furthermore, this theological framework provides a robust antidote to the previously discussed idolatry of wealth. Wealth viewed as the ultimate source of power and security easily becomes an idol. But when God, the ultimate CEO, is recognized as the source of all provision and authority, wealth is properly understood as a tool, a resource that has been entrusted to us for management. It is a means to an end, not an end in itself, preventing the corrosive effects of wealth worship and allowing us to use our financial success for godly purposes without becoming enslaved by it. We can enjoy the fruits of our labor, but our ultimate allegiance and trust remain with the divine provider.

The covenantal aspect of God's relationship with humanity also implies a commitment to justice and righteousness in our business dealings. God's covenants were not simply about blessing; they were also about establishing principles for right living. For example, the Mosaic Law contained detailed instructions for fair trade, honest weights and measures, and the protection of the vulnerable.[1] When we operate under the sovereignty of God, our enterprises are called to reflect these principles.

The entrepreneur who embraces God as CEO understands that their business is not exempt from ethical accountability to divine standards. This means they conduct business with integrity, treat employees and customers fairly, engage in responsible environmental practices, and actively seek to alleviate injustice in the marketplace and beyond.

This perspective also offers a profound source of resilience in the face of business challenges. Market downturns, unexpected failures, and competitive pressures can be devastating. However, when our ultimate security rests not in our own capabilities or the stability of the market, but in the unchanging sovereignty of God, we can face adversity with a different spirit. We can trust that even in the midst of apparent failure, God orchestrates events for purposes that may not be

---

1. Leviticus 19:35–36; Deuteronomy 24:17–22; Deuteronomy 25:13–16 (KJV).

immediately apparent. This doesn't negate the need for diligent effort and wise decision-making, but it provides an anchor of hope and a foundation of trust that transcends circumstantial outcomes.

It allows us to persevere, not out of sheer willpower, but out of a deep-seated conviction that our ultimate success is not contingent on earthly metrics, but on our faithfulness to the divine CEO. In essence, understanding God as the highest ranking official of our wealth generation efforts transforms the entire landscape of entrepreneurial wealth creation. We're called to a posture of humility, recognizing our role as stewards rather than masters, which compels us to seek divine wisdom in all our endeavors, acknowledging that true insight comes from the Creator.

Success is redefined as faithfulness to God's purposes, moving us beyond mere financial accumulation to an inspired expression of a servant-leadership model that honors the dignity of every individual within the organization. This provides a robust framework for ethical conduct, ensuring that our businesses reflect God's justice and righteousness.

This theological understanding is not a passive resignation to fate, but an active engagement with Kingdom reality, recognizing that we are co-laborers with God in the grand enterprise of His creation, called to manage His resources with integrity, wisdom, and unwavering devotion to His ultimate reign. This is the profound reimagining of Kingdom wealth: not as a personal empire to be built, but as a divinely entrusted responsibility to be faithfully stewarded in service to the One who is, and always will be, the true CEO of all.

For many, the pursuit of wealth has historically been framed by a singular objective: to possess. This drive of acquisition is the insatiable desire to accumulate more, hold tighter, and build an empire of one's own. It is a self-oriented mindset deeply ingrained in the human psyche, often amplified by societal pressures and the relentless narrative of success that equates ownership with significance. However, this perspective represents a profound misunderstanding of the true nature of Kingdom wealth.

A vision tethered to the tangible, the quantifiable, and the ultimate realization of personal gain is seen in the relentless drive to acquire assets, to expand territories, or to secure a legacy built on material holdings. Focusing on having, while not inherently sinful, can easily lead to a spiritual emptiness, a disconnect from the generative and outward-focused principles of God's economy. It fosters a sense of self-sufficiency that can border on arrogance, obscuring the fact that all we have is ultimately a trust, a temporary endowment from the divine source.

This is the "having" mentality, where value is measured by what we can claim as ours, what we can keep locked away, and can display as proof of our prosperity. It is the allure of the overflowing granary, the bursting vault, the meticulously curated collection of possessions with no thought beyond acquisition—a mentality that Jesus cautioned against.[2]

True spiritual wealth is not found in the sheer quantity of what we possess, but in our capacity to act. When we shift our perspective from mere possession to a deeper understanding of stewardship, the very definition of wealth undergoes a radical transformation. We act from a "doing and protecting" mentality in which we learn to deploy, protect, and serve others—a paradigm shift that moves us from hoarding to investing, from guarding to safeguarding, and from accumulating to contributing.

This active engagement with the resources entrusted to us is where the real value of Kingdom wealth is unleashed. It is recognizing that wealth, in its most profound sense, is not a static quantity but a dynamic force, a tool to be wielded for the advancement of God's purposes and the well-being of His creation. This is the Kingdom mindshift, one that sees wealth not as a prize to be won and kept, but as a responsibility to be exercised with wisdom and generosity.

A redefined understanding compels us to consider our role not merely as owners, but as guardians. The very act of protection

---

2. Luke 12:15–21 (KJV).

implies a value that transcends personal ownership. We protect what is precious, what is vulnerable, and that which is entrusted to our care. In the context of Kingdom wealth, this translates into a profound responsibility to safeguard not only our own assets, but also the assets of God's Kingdom.

While this includes the physical resources God has provided for the flourishing of His creation, it extends far beyond the material—encompassing the protection of human dignity, the safeguarding of justice, the defense of the vulnerable, and the preservation of the very message of the Gospel. Christian leaders operating with this "protecting" mentality understand that their wealth is a means to shield and nurture what is good and righteous, to stand as bulwarks against forces that seek to exploit or destroy. This requires discernment, courage, and a willingness to expend resources—not just for personal benefit, but for the broader cause of God's reign.

The vulnerable are a particular focal point in this reevaluation. Throughout scripture, God's heart is consistently shown to be with the marginalized, oppressed, impoverished, and voiceless. From the widow and the orphan in ancient Israel to the stranger and the prisoner in Jesus' teachings, the call to protect and advocate for those on the fringes is unequivocal. Kingdom wealth, therefore, is not truly understood or realized until it is actively directed towards the alleviation of suffering and the empowerment of the vulnerable.

It is about seeing wealth not as a personal accumulation, but as a divine provision that enables us to be instruments of rescue, provision, and restoration for those who are struggling. This goes beyond charitable donations; it involves structuring our businesses and our financial lives in ways that actively dismantle systems of oppression and create pathways for those who have been excluded or disadvantaged. This proactive stance is a commitment to use our influence and resources to build a more just and equitable world that reflects the compassionate heart of God.

Consider the implications of incorporating this protective stewardship model in our business practices. It means eschewing any business model that relies on exploitation, whether of labor, resources, or information. It demands transparency, fair dealing, and a commitment to ethical sourcing. It pushes us to invest in sustainable practices that honor the created order, rather than depleting it.

The Kingdom stewardship model encourages us to create work environments where employees are treated with respect, compensated fairly, and given opportunities for growth and dignity. It also means using our platforms to speak out against injustice and to advocate for policies that protect the vulnerable and promote the common good. This is Kingdom wealth in action, wealth that actively participates in the redemptive work of God in the world. The having mentality sees a business as a means to extract value; the protecting mentality redefines business as a means to generate and steward value for the Kingdom.

The advancement of God's Kingdom is the ultimate horizon for this redefined wealth. It is not just about personal prosperity or a generic sense of broad societal well-being. God-defined stewardship is about actively contributing to the expansion of His rule and reign in every sphere of life, including the marketplace, which means viewing our businesses as potential vehicles for demonstrating Kingdom principles—integrity, love, justice, mercy, and truth—to the world.

Our profits are not solely for personal enrichment or reinvestment, but also to be used in support of ministries, missionary endeavors, and initiatives that spread the Gospel and address the deep spiritual and physical needs of humanity. This is wealth that has an eternal perspective, wealth that is consciously aligned with God's ultimate purposes for humanity and creation. The doing and protecting aspects converge here: we actively do good works with our resources, and we protect the integrity and mission of the Kingdom by ensuring our wealth serves its agenda.

This active, protective, Kingdom-oriented approach to wealth stands in stark contrast to the often self-serving and extractive nature of wealth accumulation divorced from divine purpose. The allure of mere possession is a potent siren song, drawing individuals and enterprises into a cycle of endless acquisition that ultimately leaves them spiritually impoverished. The having mentality is inherently inward-looking, focused on building walls rather than bridges, on securing a personal fort rather than engaging in the broader mission field. It is a self-perpetuating chase that never reaches a satisfying conclusion, a hunger that cannot be sated by accumulation alone—a static understanding of wealth that fails to recognize its God-given potential for dynamic impact and transformative service.

WHILE THE PRECEDING DISCUSSIONS HAVE LAID THE theological groundwork, it is through examining specific lives that these principles gain tangible form and inspiration. The biblical narrative is replete with individuals whose lives exemplify this shift from possession to protection, from accumulation to active stewardship for a higher purpose. These are not merely cautionary tales of avarice, but powerful illustrations of how wealth, when rightly understood and deployed, can become a potent force for good, a catalyst for the Kingdom's expansion, and a testament to God's transformative power. The narratives demonstrate that true wealth is not measured by what we hoard, but by what we are empowered to do, by what we are called to protect, and by whose Kingdom we ultimately serve.

Transitioning from a "having" to a "doing and protecting" mindset is not merely a theoretical exercise; it is a call to practical discipleship within the realm of finance and enterprise. Moving beyond the accumulation of capital as an end in itself and embracing wealth as a trust turns wealth into a powerful tool to be wielded in alignment with divine mandates. This requires a fundamental reorientation of our values, a willingness to relinquish the intoxicating grip of personal ownership in favor of the liberating responsibility of stewardship. It means understanding that the true measure of our affluence is not in the breadth of our possessions, but in the depth of our impact—our capacity to be a force for good, to stand as guardians of the vulnerable, and to become active participants in the unfolding purposes of God's eternal Kingdom.

This is the essence of Kingdom wealth, a concept that transcends the limitations of earthly economics and points towards an enduring and infinitely more valuable reality.

SIX
THE ARIMATHEAN BLUEPRINT
SACRIFICIAL STEWARDSHIP IN ACTION

From the shadows of Scripture, certain figures step forward—not with booming pronouncements or earth-shattering miracles, but with quiet, decisive actions that reveal profound truths about discipleship and stewardship. Joseph of Arimathea is such a figure in the annals of Christian history.

Often relegated to a mere footnote in the Passion narrative, Joseph's presence at the crucifixion and his subsequent role in the burial of Jesus speak to a different kind of wealth: influence, courage, and sacrificial giving, wielded by a man of considerable means within the complex socio-political landscape of Roman Judea. To understand Joseph of Arimathea is to gain a deeper appreciation for how Kingdom principles can be lived out, even—and especially—within the halls of power and affluence.

The historical context of Roman Judea during the time of Jesus was precarious. Roman occupation exerted immense pressure on the local Jewish population, creating a delicate balance of power and influence. Within this environment, individuals of significant status, like Joseph, had to navigate carefully. The Jewish high court, known as the Sanhedrin, held considerable authority, but it operated under the ultimate dominion of Rome. To be a member of this council meant being a man of elite standing and likely substantial wealth.

Joseph's standing as a prominent member of the Sanhedrin[1] suggests not only respect, but responsibility and connection to the established order. He was not a man operating on the fringes; he was an insider, someone who understood the intricacies of law, custom, and governance. His resources were not merely personal possessions; they represented a network of influence and a tangible stake in the prevailing social structure.

His decision to approach Pontius Pilate, the Roman governor, for the body of Jesus was an act of remarkable courage and strategic astuteness. The crucifixion of a condemned criminal was a brutal and public spectacle, designed to instill fear and reinforce Rome's authority. Bodies were often left to be scavenged by animals or subjected to ignominious burial.[2] By intervening in such a process, Joseph associated himself with One whose followers were scattered and whose movement appeared to be crushed.

Joseph's actions reveal a man who actively participated in the

---

1. Mark 15:43 (NKJV).
2. Bart D. Ehrman, "Did Romans Allow Decent Burials for Crucified Criminals?," *The Bart Ehrman Blog*, July 24, 2023, accessed March 2, 2026, https://ehrmanblog.org/did-romans-allow-decent-burials-for-crucified-criminals/.

unfolding drama of redemption. He understood the implications of his request. At a moment when such an association was most dangerous, asking for the body of Jesus—even discreetly—was a public acknowledgment of Him. This was not a casual act of charity, but a deliberate decision that carried significant social—and potentially political—ramifications for a man of his wealth and standing.

The Gospels tell us that Joseph owned a tomb, a *new* tomb, "which he had hewn out of the rock."[3] A tomb hewn from rock was a significant investment, a testament to his wealth and foresight. This was no common grave or temporary resting place. It signified permanence, respect, and a dedication to burial rites deeply integral to Jewish tradition.

The emphasis on the tomb's newness is significant. It suggests that it was a prized possession, reserved perhaps for Joseph or his family, a place of honor. Joseph did not simply provide a burial spot for Jesus; he offered his best—a resting place of security and dignity for Jesus' body. At a moment when Jesus had no earthly possessions or kingdom to offer His followers, Joseph's actions speak volumes about his understanding of true worth—a valuation that transcended the fleeting nature of earthly power and possessions.

3. Matthew 27:60; Mark 15:46; Luke 23:53 (NKJV).

For an influential member of the Sanhedrin, taking responsibility for the body of one crucified as a criminal and placing Him in a tomb from his own plot was a significant risk. Even Jesus' known disciples had fled. Joseph understood that his request could alienate him from his peers, jeopardize his reputation, and perhaps even bring repercussions against him from the Roman authorities. Providing his tomb was an intentional investment in a cause that, at that moment, seemed lost. In that very act, Joseph of Arimathea wielded his wealth as a tool of profound discipleship, enabling him to act when others could—or would—not. Such an action required moral courage, deep conviction, and a willingness to stand with the condemned when all others had fled.

This highlights a crucial dimension of stewardship: the willingness to use one's most valued possessions for the purposes of God's Kingdom. True stewardship is not merely giving from surplus; it is the reordering of our personal priorities and the radical alignment of material wealth with spiritual conviction. Joseph's tangible expression of faith demonstrates that his primary allegiance lay not with Rome or the Sanhedrin, but with the crucified Nazarene.

This sets a powerful precedent for Kingdom entrepreneurs who operate within secular structures. Joseph did not abandon the system in which he lived; he acted faithfully within it. He used neither prudence as an excuse for silence nor his position as a shield against costly obedience. Instead, he leveraged influence and wealth in service to a higher loyalty. His example shows that resources can be wielded for the Kingdom not only in overtly religious settings, but within the very systems and structures of the world.

THE NARRATIVE OF JOSEPH OF ARIMATHEA THEREFORE challenges modern perceptions of wealth as merely an instrument for personal gain, comfort, or status. His story shows how wealth, when coupled with spiritual insight and courage, can become a force for compassion, dignity, and faithful action in the face of overwhelming opposition.

Joseph also safeguarded the mission itself. By ensuring Jesus received a proper burial, he protected more than a body. He protected the dignity of the Lord, the fragile hope of the followers, and the integrity of the story at a moment when all appeared lost. Had Jesus' body been left exposed or discarded in disgrace, the visual narrative would have been one of total defeat. Joseph's action created a place where grief, reverence, and ultimately resurrection hope could converge.[4]

That principle carries forward into the marketplace. Enterprises with strong ethical or spiritual foundations will face moments when the mission itself is vulnerable—pressured by crisis, compromise, or cultural hostility. In those moments, leadership must do more than preserve operations; it must guard the soul of the organization by actively reinforcing

4. Matthew 28:1–5; Mark 16:1–8; Luke 24:1–12 (NKJV).

the values, relationships, and commitments without which outward success becomes hollow.

The urgency inherent in Joseph of Arimathea's actions offers another powerful lens through which to examine leadership. Jesus had been crucified, and the Sabbath was approaching rapidly. Time was not an abstract concern; it was a spiritual and practical constraint. If Joseph was going to act, he had to do so quickly. He embodied a "first responder" mentality. In the immediate aftermath of the crucifixion, he didn't wait for instructions, formal approvals, or a more convenient time. He acted.

> Joseph of Arimathea, a prominent council member, who was himself waiting for the Kingdom of God, coming and taking courage, went in to Pilate and asked for the body of Jesus.
>
> MARK 15:43 NKJV

Joseph's courageous actions flowed from his conviction. He was waiting for the Kingdom of God. His spiritual expectancy translated into practical readiness. He did not make a casual request—it was a deliberate, bold move requiring him to step out of the shadows, leverage his position, and confront authority directly. His standing, resources, and courage were already available to God when the decisive moment came. He recognized a sacred crisis and understood that delay would mean dishonor.

In business, such moments may appear as sudden instability, moral crisis, employee hardship, community disruption, or threats to the organization's integrity. Enterprises shaped by Kingdom values must cultivate the ability to respond swiftly, ethically, and sacrificially when the stakes are high. For leaders today, this means building organizations whose values are not decorative, but operational—embedded deeply enough that when the critical moment arrives, the response is swift and aligned.

This is the essence of first responder stewardship: in moments of vulnerability, decisive leaders do not merely observe events unfolding; they move toward the place of need. It is not merely reactive; it is the fruit of prior formation—what happens when conviction has already shaped the leader long before the crisis arrives.

THE *NEWNESS* OF JOSEPH'S TOMB REMAINS ONE OF THE MOST significant details in the narrative. It implies that he offered something pristine, valuable, and likely reserved for himself or his household. This is the heart of sacrificial stewardship: not offering the leftovers, but dedicating one's best.

In the business world, success is often measured by curated displays of wealth—prime real estate, luxurious vehicles and amenities, elite access, impressive portfolios, and other outward indicators of status. These things can become shorthand for legacy. Yet the Arimathean blueprint invites a radical redefinition. Joseph's legacy was not secured by preserving his asset, but by surrendering it into God's redemptive story.

Kingdom legacy is not a monument to self, but a contribution to something eternal. For Christian business leaders, this raises difficult but necessary questions. What are our "new tombs"? What are the most valuable assets, opportunities, relationships, or forms of influence entrusted to us? Are we willing to dedicate these not merely to personal comfort or institutional prestige, but to the protection of the vulnerable, the strengthening of mission, and the advancement of God's purposes?

This does not mean rejecting success or scorning wise provision. It means refusing to let comfort define our calling. Are we willing to dedicate our efforts to alleviating suffering, advancing justice, or supporting the marginalized? It means understanding that true wealth is not measured by what we retain, but by what we are willing to release in obedience. Joseph's act challenges leaders to see their assets not as trophies of achievement, but as instruments of stewardship.

The lure of luxury can be subtle. It whispers that hard work entitles us to excess, that visible prosperity proves success, and that preserving our own comfort is wisdom. Yet Joseph's example points in another direction. He chose to invest his most valuable earthly possession in a cause that offered no immediate worldly return. In doing so, he demonstrated that wealth reaches its highest purpose not in self-display, but in sacrificial usefulness. Are we equally willing to invest in initiatives that might not have immediate or obvious financial returns, but that align with a higher purpose?

For enterprises that claim Kingdom orientation, this means cultivating a culture that prizes generosity over ostentation, service over self-indulgence, and purpose over prestige. It means that when decisions about resource allocation arise, the governing question is not simply, "What benefits us most?" but, "What most faithfully serves the purposes of God?" This could involve investing in training programs for disadvantaged youth, developing affordable housing solutions, or creating innovative solutions for environmental challenges that disproportionately affect the poor.

Joseph's sacrifice was not an incidental gesture. It was a defining act that revealed what he truly valued. His offering of the tomb became part of a story far greater than his own biography. That is the essence of Kingdom wealth: a legacy built not on the accumulation of luxury, but on courageous participation in God's unfolding purposes.

In essence, Joseph of Arimathea's quiet intervention was an act of profound strategic stewardship. He understood, perhaps more clearly than many around him, that the treatment of Jesus' body had direct implications for the dignity, continuity, and credibility of the mission. By securing the tomb, he was not merely performing a burial rite. He was fortifying the bedrock upon which hope would stand.

This lesson remains critical for modern business leaders: move beyond superficial acts of charity and embrace valiant forms of generosity that invest in the marginalized members of society, committing resources to the integrity and continuation of endeavors that reflect God's values. Protecting the mission is not an optional add-on; it is a strategic and spiritual imperative. It demands foresight, courage, and a willingness to deploy resources—even treasured personal resources—to ensure that what God has entrusted remains uncorrupted, undefiled, and capable of advancing His purposes.

When it is viewed not as a one-time event but as a pivotal turning point, Joseph's sacrifice reveals the true Arimathean blueprint: wealth submitted to God with courageous conviction, measured not by what is preserved for self but by what is surrendered for the sake of His Kingdom. As we apply this to our enterprises, we begin to embody the essence of Kingdom wealth—a legacy built on preserving and strengthening the body of Christ.

SEVEN
THE QUADRUPLE BOTTOM LINE
PEOPLE, PLANET, PROFITABILITY, ETERNITY

The conventional wisdom of the modern business world often distills success down to a single, potent metric: profit. The financial bottom line reigns as the primary barometer by which companies are judged, investors are wooed, and leaders are applauded. Undeniably, financial growth is essential to the sustainability and growth of any enterprise. However, from a Kingdom perspective, it is not the full measure of success.

Our previous exploration of Joseph of Arimathea's sacrificial stewardship underscored a deeper principle: true wealth and legacy are not defined solely by material accumulation or personal comfort, but by the wise and generous deployment of resources for an eternally greater purpose. This same principle must extend to how we define entrepreneurial success. A Kingdom-oriented business, by its very nature, must transcend the confines of financial reporting and embrace a more expansive understanding of its impact and responsibilities.

This is where the Quadruple Bottom Line emerges as a vital framework for Kingdom entrepreneurs. It intentionally expands the traditional single bottom line by demonstrating that business success is not merely financial, but multifaceted. This is not a feel-good addition to a mission statement, but a strategic, fundamental reorientation of business strategy rooted in Kingdom stewardship. A truly successful enterprise accounts for its impact on people, the planet, profit, and its ultimate contribution to an eternal purpose. If we are indeed stewards of God's resources, then our accountability extends to all the domains for which He has expressed concern.

The traditional business model is a relentless drive for profit maximization. Efficiency, innovation, and market share—crucial components of this pursuit—are valued as instruments toward financial gain. When viewed as the sole measure of success, the pursuit of profit can lean toward ethical compromise, environmental degradation, and a disregard for the well-being of individuals and communities.

Industries that prioritize short-term profits over long-term sustainability often produce negative outcomes, such as exploitation of labor, depletion of natural resources, and social inequalities. Such a narrow focus blinds leaders to the broader consequences of their decisions, severing business operations from the holistic concerns of a Creator.

The Quadruple Bottom Line offers a powerful antidote to this narrow vision. It proposes the notion that a

Kingdom business must thrive across four interconnected dimensions: People, Planet, Profit, and Eternity. These dimensions provide a practical lens through which Kingdom entrepreneurs can evaluate the true impact of their enterprise.

1. People (Social Capital): The biblical call to love our neighbors as ourselves urges businesses to consider the impact of their decisions on others, ensuring their operations contribute to human flourishing rather than exploitation. A business must recognize its impact on the dignity of every person it touches—employees, customers, suppliers, and the community. Kingdom entrepreneurs recognize every individual's inherent worth, measuring success not only by productivity, but by whether the enterprise fosters fairness, development, trust, and a commitment to the well-being of all stakeholders.

This commitment begins with ethical employment practices that extend beyond legal compliance. Labor laws establish a necessary baseline; however, Kingdom entrepreneurs are called to embody deeper principles of justice, fairness, and generosity. Fair wages, safe working conditions, and opportunities for advancement are not merely corporate policies; they are expressions of respect for the God-given worth of every individual. When employees are treated with dignity and integrity, the workplace becomes more than an economic system—it becomes a community in which people are able to grow, contribute, and flourish.

Employees are not static resources but individuals with talents, aspirations, and potential waiting to be cultivated.

Kingdom-oriented enterprises also recognize the importance of investing in the development and well-being of their people. Businesses that provide meaningful opportunities for training, mentorship, and professional growth demonstrate a commitment to long-term stewardship of human potential. Such investment benefits both the individual and the organization, fostering innovation, loyalty, and deeper engagement.

Beyond professional development, a people-centered culture must address the broader well-being of those within the organization. Physical, emotional, and mental health all contribute to the flourishing of individuals and the health of the workplace. Compassionate policies—such as flexible scheduling, wellness initiatives, or supportive leave practices—communicate that employees are valued as whole persons rather than merely as contributors to productivity. This holistic approach reflects the biblical vision of human well-being, which encompasses the whole person: spirit, soul, and body (1 Thessalonians 5:23).

The ripple effects of a people-first culture extend beyond the internal structure of the organization. Businesses do not exist in isolation; they operate within communities that shape and sustain them. Kingdom entrepreneurs therefore recognize a responsibility to contribute positively to the social fabric around them. This may include supporting local initiatives, partnering with community organizations, or creating opportunities that strengthen the well-being of the neighborhoods in which the business operates. In doing so, the enterprise participates in the biblical mandate to "seek the welfare of the city" (Jeremiah 29:7).

It is important to note that prioritizing people is not merely an ethical aspiration; it is also a strategic advantage. Organizations that cultivate trust, fairness, and respect often experience higher levels of employee engagement, greater innovation, and stronger customer relationships. Reduced turnover, increased productivity, and a positive reputation frequently follow. When employees feel valued and aligned with the mission of the organization, their commitment deepens, strengthening the enterprise from within.

Ultimately, a people-first approach reflects the heart of Kingdom leadership. It views individuals not as means to an end, but as neighbors to be loved and partners in a shared mission. Businesses that embrace this perspective cultivate workplaces characterized by dignity, service, and mutual respect. In such environments, human potential is not merely utilized—it is nurtured and multiplied, contributing to both organizational strength and the broader flourishing of society.

2. Planet (Environmental Stewardship):

The stewardship of creation forms the second pillar of the Quadruple Bottom Line. Scripture consistently presents the Earth as the handiwork of God, entrusted to humanity's care. From the opening chapters of Genesis, humanity is commissioned to "care for and maintain it" (Genesis 2:15 NET). This mandate establishes our framework of responsibility: as stewards, we are charged to manage the

Earth's resources for future generations. A Kingdom business must regard creation as a sacred trust. Our leadership role is one that demonstrates to the rest of the world how God wants His planet to be treated.

For Kingdom entrepreneurs, environmental responsibility therefore moves beyond regulatory compliance or corporate image management. It becomes an expression of obedience and reverence toward the Creator. Businesses must recognize that the health of the planet is inseparable from the flourishing of the communities they serve. Economic activity that damages ecosystems ultimately undermines the stability upon which society—and commerce itself—depends.

Practically, this commitment calls business leaders to examine their environmental footprint and pursue sustainable practices wherever possible. Responsible resource management may include reducing waste, improving energy efficiency, adopting renewable energy sources, or redesigning production systems to minimize environmental impact. Increasingly, forward-thinking companies are embracing circular economic models that seek to reduce unnecessary consumption and extend the useful life of materials.

Creation stewardship can also become a catalyst for innovation. When businesses commit to sustainable practices, they often discover new efficiencies, technologies, and opportunities for improvement. Renewable energy systems, sustainable supply chains, and environmentally responsible design are not merely ethical choices; they frequently lead to long-term resilience and operational stability.

Moreover, caring for creation is not limited to minimizing harm. Kingdom stewardship invites businesses to participate actively in restoration. Whether through conservation efforts, responsible land management, or investment in environmental solutions, enterprises can contribute to the renewal and protection of the natural world. Such efforts reflect the biblical vision of creation itself awaiting restoration (Romans 8:19–22).

When businesses embrace environmental stewardship, they demonstrate that economic activity and creation care are not adversaries. Rather, responsible enterprises recognize that the prosperity of people, the health of the planet, and the sustainability of business are deeply interconnected. In honoring creation, Kingdom business leaders ultimately honor the Creator—contributing to a future in which both humanity and the Earth may flourish.

3. Profit (Long-term Financial Impact): Within the QBL framework, profit—while not the sole objective—is the engine that enables broader impact. A business that lacks financial stability cannot sustain operations, provide employment, or invest in its mission—however, the destination is far more significant than the engine itself.

The critical distinction lies in how profit is understood. In conventional business models, profit is often treated as the ultimate goal toward which all activity is directed. In the Kingdom framework, however, profitability becomes a means rather than an end. Financial success enables the enterprise to expand its positive influence, invest in its people, steward creation responsibly, and pursue initiatives that reflect God's purposes.

In the workings of a Kingdom business, it is understood that acquiring wealth is not evil. Instead, we learn to align our pursuit and application of wealth with divine principles. Scripture frequently affirms the value of wise stewardship and diligent management of resources. Proverbs praises the disciplined and prudent, recognizing that financial stability contributes to both personal and communal well-being. For Kingdom entrepreneurs, sound financial management therefore reflects a commitment to responsible stewardship rather than the pursuit of wealth for its own sake.

Businesses that operate with integrity and purpose find that profitability often becomes more sustainable over time. Companies that invest in employee well-being, treat customers honestly, and steward resources responsibly tend to build trust and long-term loyalty. These factors strengthen organizational resilience and often lead to greater stability during economic challenges.

Financial stewardship also shapes how profits are used. Kingdom-oriented enterprises recognize that revenue can become a powerful instrument for advancing good. Profits may be reinvested in employee development, community initiatives, charitable efforts, or innovations that address pressing societal needs. In this way, financial success becomes a resource that fuels broader impact.

An ethically-managed business can be a powerful force for good, when guided by wisdom, integrity, and Kingdom values. Financial success becomes more than a measure of performance—it becomes a tool through which enterprises can serve people, care for creation, and contribute to purposes that extend far beyond the marketplace.

4. Eternity (Spiritual and Purposeful Impact): The final dimension of the Quadruple Bottom Line brings the entire framework into its ultimate perspective: eternity. Beyond people, planet, and profit lies the question of eternal purpose. How does this enterprise reflect God's character, advance His purposes, and build a legacy that outlives market performance? This dimension encourages leaders to ask how their business can be a tangible expression of God's love and truth in the marketplace, thereby glorifying Him.

From a Kingdom perspective, the work of business cannot be separated from the broader narrative of redemption. Enterprises shape communities, influence culture, and affect countless lives. When guided by Kingdom values, businesses become instruments through which justice, compassion, and restoration can be expressed in the marketplace.

This eternal perspective invites leaders to reconsider the meaning of success. The achievements most celebrated in the commercial world—market share, brand recognition, financial growth—are inherently temporary. Scripture reminds us that earthly treasures are fragile, while investments aligned with God's purposes endure beyond the present age (Matthew

6:19–21). The true legacy of a business therefore lies not only in what it builds economically, but in the lives it touches and the values it embodies.

A Kingdom enterprise can influence eternity in several ways. It may create workplaces where integrity, service, and respect are practiced daily. It may foster environments in which individuals experience encouragement, dignity, and spiritual growth. Leaders who conduct business with humility, compassion, and ethical conviction often become living testimonies to the transforming power of faith.

Businesses can also participate in God's redemptive work through the way they deploy their resources and influence. Enterprises that alleviate suffering, serve underserved communities, or promote justice contribute meaningfully to the healing of broken systems. In these moments, commerce becomes more than economic exchange; it becomes participation in God's restorative purposes.

The question of eternal impact also shapes how leaders make difficult decisions. Opportunities that promise financial gain may sometimes require ethical compromise. A leader who operates with an eternal perspective weighs such choices differently, recognizing that integrity, faithfulness, and obedience to God carry greater value than short-term profit.

For the Kingdom entrepreneur, the eternity bottom line ultimately reframes the purpose of enterprise itself. Business becomes more than a mechanism for generating wealth; it becomes a platform through which God's character can be reflected in the world. When leaders steward their influence in this way, they build legacies that reach far beyond balance sheets and market cycles.

Eternal success is not measured in quantifiable financial terms, but in the qualitative influence the business has on people's lives, its role in demonstrating God's character through its operations, and its contribution to a broader redemptive narrative. In the end, the most enduring measure of success is not how large a company becomes, but how faithfully it contributes to the advancement of God's purposes. A legacy of eternal significance extends beyond material wealth and worldly recognition. Enterprises that embrace this perspective discover that their work participates in a story far greater than commerce alone—a story whose significance echoes into eternity.

THE INTEGRATION OF THESE FOUR BOTTOM LINES REQUIRES A profound shift in mindset—calling leaders to move from a profit-centric model to one that is holistic, ethical, and purpose-driven. That shift is not always easy. It may require costly choices, slower gains, or decisions that do not maximize short-term return. Yet the dimensions of the Quadruple Bottom Line are not enemies of one another. They are deeply interconnected. Over time, a business that genuinely values people, stewards creation, sustains profit wisely, and remains anchored in eternal purpose will prove to be stronger, more resilient, and more credible than one built on financial gain alone.

This framework is the essence of Kingdom entrepreneurship: building financially sound, morally grounded enterprises that are socially responsible, environmentally faithful, and eternally conscious.

As we move with God, beyond the limited metrics of the financial world, we learn how to embrace a more comprehensive understanding of value creation—which is true success in the business context. That is our call as Kingdom entrepreneurs: to steward business in a way that honors God, blesses humanity, cares for the earth, and contributes to a legacy that endures beyond the temporal for the advancement of His eternal purposes in the earth.

EIGHT
SERVANT-HEARTED LEADERSHIP
THE FOUNDATION OF KINGDOM ENTERPRISE

The prevailing paradigms of leadership in the secular world often mirror hierarchical systems rooted in ancient imperial or military models of control, authority, and positional power. Leaders are frequently defined by their ability to dominate, command, and enforce obedience, wielding power as a means to extract compliance—as if authority were an inherent right of position rather than a delegated responsibility.

In this model, the leader stands at the apex—elevated above the structure, often disconnected from the lived realities of those beneath—while success is measured by control, output, and the consistent execution of directives. Though such systems may achieve short-term efficiency, they often do so at the expense of human flourishing, fostering a dynamic in which the primary focus shifts toward personal gain, status, and the exercise of authority. Rather than recognizing individuals as valued contributors, this produces a work culture often marked by fear, competition, resentment, and a lack of genuine engagement—like cogs in a machine rather than participants in a shared mission. This inherently transactional environment ultimately leaves a void, exposing a deeper human need for connection, purpose, and genuine care.

In stark contrast, Jesus Christ introduced a model of leadership that remains profoundly countercultural. In Mark 10:45, He declared, *"For even the Son of Man did not come to be served, but to serve, and to give his life as a ransom for many."* This was not merely a statement—it was the governing principle of His life and ministry. Rather than accumulating what the culture regarded as power, Jesus demonstrated that true authority and power is revealed through humility, service, and selfless living. He did not lead from a distance, but entered into the lives and struggles of those He led, showing empathy and a commitment to their well-being that transcended all conventional leadership expectations. His leadership was not rooted in position, but in moral authority—established through sacrifice, integrity, and a love dedicated to the well-being of others.

This radical inversion of the prevailing power structures offers a glimpse into the very nature of God's Kingdom—a realm where true greatness is measured not by the ability to command, but by the willingness to serve. Such a paradigm challenges the foundation of conventional leadership, calling into question systems built solely on performance and control. In their place, it offers a vision of leadership grounded in purpose, relationship, and the fruitful lives of those they lead.

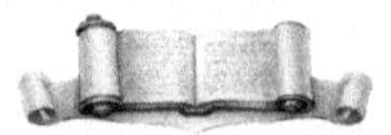

THE PIVOTAL MOMENT THAT VIVIDLY ILLUSTRATES SERVANT-hearted leadership is found in John 13. Fully aware that the Father had given all things into His hands, and that He had come from God and was returning to God, Jesus rose from supper, laid aside His outer garments, took a towel, and wrapped it around His waist. He then poured water into a basin and began to wash the disciples' feet, drying them with the towel He wore. In the cultural context of that time, foot washing was performed as an act of profound humility and sanitation, and an essential ritual of hospitality. The master of the house would never undertake this task for his guests, let alone his own disciples—this task was assigned to the lowest servants.

However, Jesus, in an unmistakable demonstration of kingly leadership, dismantled assumptive and prideful ideas about status, ambition, and elevation by deliberately assuming the position of a servant. In doing so, He redefined authority and power as the responsibility to serve—leading by honoring His team, becoming the source of service, and expressing true leadership through humility, proximity, and selfless generosity.

Jesus made His meaning clear, leaving nothing open to interpretation: *"You call me Teacher and Lord, and you are right to do so, for that is what I am. So if I, your Lord and Teacher, have washed your feet, you also ought to wash one another's feet. For I have given you an example, that you also should do as I have done to you."*[1] This is a direct mandate, a charge to His followers to emulate His leadership style. It is a call to service, a directive to prioritize the needs of others, to humble oneself for the sake of uplifting and caring for those under one's charge.

The Lord's radical example reverses secular power dynamics, where leaders control resources and dictate outcomes, while subordinates seek favor. In a Kingdom enterprise, leadership is a transformative shift in the heart that manifests through actions. This requires leaders to reevaluate their identity from "boss" to "servant." A servant's heart defines how leaders give and faithfully serve stakeholders, replacing secular expectations that focus on self-serving.

Within this model, leaders are the chief servants of the organization, prioritizing the well-being of their team over their own. They are the ones most willing to bear burdens, engage difficulty, actively seeking to understand employees' challenges, offering support and resources to foster a safe, valued, and empowered environment. Leaders who engage with their staff with awareness, presence, and care lift others towards strength and maturity, supporting the spiritual, emotional, and overall well-being of every individual within the organization.

They view the people in their organization as unique individuals with gifts, aspirations, and vulnerabilities, each

1. John 13:13-15 (NKJV).

created in God's image. Their primary responsibility shifts from maximizing shareholder value in a purely financial sense, to maximizing human flourishing within the context of the enterprise—operating with integrity and a commitment to ethical excellence.

This stands in stark contrast to leadership styles that emphasize distance, delegation of blame, and a focus on individual accomplishment at the expense of team cohesion. Jesus, however, demonstrated that true power is found in voluntary submission to the needs of others. By washing His disciples' feet, He willingly stepped into a position of humility, revealing a kind of power that cannot be overthrown or replicated by earthly systems. This power is rooted in love, sacrifice, and an unwavering commitment to the well-being of others. It is a power that transforms, builds, and endures.

For a Kingdom enterprise, this redefines authority. It is no longer derived from title or position, but from a demonstrated commitment to serve. Respect and loyalty are not demanded—they are cultivated through consistent acts of integrity, care, and sacrifice. In this way, leadership produces a culture of mutual honor and shared responsibility. This servant-hearted model also reframes how resources are stewarded. Leadership is not driven by the pursuit of profit alone, but by a commitment to glorify God and benefit humanity. This may require decisions that are not immediately lucrative, yet uphold ethical standards, promote fairness, and contribute to the common good. Whether through investing in sustainable practices, ensuring just compensation, or prioritizing people over short-term gain, Kingdom leaders operate from an eternal perspective. The focus shifts from maximizing return for shareholders to cultivating lasting value for all stakeholders—reflecting the priorities of the Kingdom of God and establishing a foundation of lasting trust and integrity.

Jesus' act of washing His disciples' feet also establishes a practical standard: no task is beneath a true leader when it serves the needs of others. In a culture where leadership can become synonymous with distance and control, His example calls leaders to remain engaged, present, and willing—meaning we willingly roll up our sleeves, get our hands dirty, and step directly into the work that needs to be done. This does not imply micromanagement, but it does require participation. A servant leader is willing to step into difficulty, share in responsibility, and to understand the realities faced at every level of the organization. This type of leadership fosters trust and a sense of shared ownership and purpose. When leaders exhibit this kind of humility, it creates team solidarity. It communicates that every role is valued—and that leadership is not removed from the work, but invested in the success and strength of every individual.

WHEN LEADERS FOSTER AN ENVIRONMENT WHERE vulnerability is viewed as a powerful catalyst for growth and innovation, they empower their team. Shifting from a model of command and control to one that prioritizes service and empowerment requires more than structural change—it demands transformation. This is not merely an operational adjustment; it is a redefinition of strength, authority, and influence. In a Kingdom enterprise, leadership is expressed through the deliberate distribution of influence and the intentional development of others. True strength is revealed in the ability to equip others, entrust responsibility, and create space for people to grow into their full capacity.

Creating a culture of psychological safety is the bedrock upon which this empowerment is built. At its core is an environment where people can contribute, develop, and take ownership of their work without fear. When individuals are no longer governed by the pressure of perfection or the fear of failure, they engage more fully, think more clearly, and participate more meaningfully in the mission.

When leaders demonstrate humility—acknowledging what they do not know, admitting missteps, and remaining open to input—they establish a tone that invites growth across the organization. Rather than presenting themselves as infallible, they model a posture of continual learning. This creates space for others to do the same, fostering an environment where progress is valued over perfection.

This does not imply indecision or a lack of direction. A leader may say, *"I'm not entirely sure of the best way to approach this new market strategy, and I value your insight."* Such openness invites collaboration while reinforcing trust in the team's collective wisdom. In doing so, leadership becomes more human, more relational, and ultimately more effective.

Communication sustains this culture. Servant leaders do not merely give direction—they cultivate dialogue. They listen with intention, seek understanding before responding, and establish clear pathways for feedback. Whether through structured forums (town hall meetings, anonymous feedback channels, or dedicated idea platforms), communication remains open, consistent, and purposeful. Just as importantly, leaders respond with transparency. When people see that their input is acknowledged and considered, trust deepens and engagement strengthens.

Empowerment is most clearly expressed through the responsible delegation of authority. This extends beyond assigning tasks; it involves entrusting individuals and teams with ownership and decision-making within defined boundaries. While micromanagement controls process, servant leadership provides vision, establishes expectations, and allows others to determine how best to execute. In doing so, leaders cultivate both competence and confidence, creating space for innovation to emerge from those closest to the work.

The result is a workforce that is innovative, engaged, and resilient. When individuals feel trusted, they take initiative. When their contributions are valued, their commitment soars. Innovation becomes a natural outcome of an environment where people are free to think, experiment, and refine without fear. Rather than operating under pressure, teams begin to function with purpose, ownership, and a shared investment in the mission.

Strength in vulnerability, as exemplified by Christ, extends to the leader's personal interactions. When leaders openly acknowledge their mistakes—such as admitting after a failed project, *"My initial directive was too restrictive and hindered your progress. I take responsibility for not allowing for more flexibility"*—they demonstrate accountability and maturity. This posture disarms defensiveness and creates an environment conducive to collective growth. In contrast, leadership that deflects responsibility breeds fear, stifles communication, and erodes trust.

Servant-hearted leadership is relational. Jesus led through connection, knowing His followers' strengths, struggles, fears, and potential. He corrected, challenged, and encouraged them, committed to their growth. A trusting team is better equipped to weather storms, learn from failure, and adapt to change. Kingdom leaders are therefore called to move beyond surface interaction and intentionally invest in people—cultivating environments marked by empathy, active listening, and genuine care, where individuals feel seen, heard, and valued.

This relational depth strengthens teams, reinforcing unity within organizations that equip each person to navigate challenges with resilience. Leaders who commit to developing people rather than merely directing them create cultures that are both strong and sustainable. It is a mark of true maturity and spiritual grounding when leaders derive satisfaction not from being the source of all action, but from facilitating the brilliance and contribution of others.

Mirroring the very nature of God's relational and empowering Kingdom, this model ultimately redefines how influence is exercised. Leadership is no longer about control, but about cultivation. It transforms the workplace from a hierarchical structure into a dynamic ecosystem of shared responsibility, mutual respect, and collective growth.

Jesus exemplified this kind of authority. His leadership was defined by love and sacrificial service, not coercion or control. His authority drew people—it did not force them. In the same way, Kingdom leaders inspire rather than intimidate, equip rather than dominate, and build rather than manipulate.

Applying the principle of *"loving your neighbor as yourself"* means extending the same grace and understanding to colleagues that we would desire for ourselves. Leadership is not about being the source of all solutions, but about developing the capacity of others. The measure of success is not merely organizational performance, but the growth of the people within it.

In this way, leadership contributes not only to the success of the enterprise, but to the fruitful lives of those they lead—establishing a culture that multiplies strength, honors people, and reflects the values of God's Kingdom in every operation.

THIS EMPATHETIC APPROACH IS ESSENTIAL FOR FOSTERING reconciliation, demonstrating a commitment to addressing the whole person—not just the immediate issue. It acknowledges that individuals are not merely resources or problem-solvers, but people with depth, complexity, and inherent value.

> Now all things *are* of God, who has reconciled us to Himself through Jesus Christ, and has given us the ministry of reconciliation, 19 that is, that God was in Christ reconciling the world to Himself, not imputing their trespasses to them, and has committed to us the word of reconciliation. 20 Now then, we are ambassadors for Christ, as though God were pleading through us: we implore *you* on Christ's behalf, be reconciled to God.
>
> 2 CORINTHIANS 5:18-20

The biblical mandate for reconciliation, as outlined in 2 Corinthians 5:18–20, is not merely theological—it is deeply practical. It calls leaders to pursue restoration, to mend relationships, and to build bridges where division has occurred. Reconciliation often requires courage: the willingness to confront truth, admit fault, apologize when necessary, and facilitate meaningful resolution. It also calls for vulnerability. Rather than assigning blame, servant-hearted leaders guide teams toward understanding, correction, and relational repair. In doing so, conflict becomes not a point of fracture, but an opportunity for alignment and growth.

Integrity anchors this process. While grace and empathy are essential, they must be grounded in truth. Leaders must not shy away from the facts; it is imperative that they assess situations honestly, make decisions based on what is right rather than convenient, and address shortcomings with a commitment to development—not condemnation. This balance of truth and grace reflects the very character of God and defines the standard of Kingdom leadership.

When leaders respond with composure, humility, and a commitment to resolution, they help form a culture where these behaviors are multiplied. Emotional discipline, thoughtful response, and a peacemaker's posture cultivate trust and psychological safety throughout the organization.

At the same time, Kingdom leadership does not sacrifice clarity for harmony. Resolution must ultimately produce direction. Decisions must be made, communicated, and implemented with integrity—ensuring that both relational health and organizational effectiveness remain aligned. In this way, leadership reflects both compassion and conviction.

Wise leaders establish environments that minimize unnecessary conflict. They maintain emotional regulation, pause before responding, and strive to approach the situation with the mindset of a peacemaker. Personal discipline is not about suppressing emotions but about channeling them constructively, allowing them to inform rather than dictate one's actions. It requires a deep awareness of one's own triggers and a conscious effort to respond in alignment with Kingdom values. When leaders consistently model this behavior, they cultivate an environment where healthy conflict resolution becomes the norm throughout the organization.

Through clear expectations, open communication, and intentional development of interpersonal skills, they create cultures where collaboration thrives. This reflects the principle of loving one's neighbor—not only in response to conflict, but in the prevention of it.

Ultimately, navigating conflict with grace and integrity reveals the true substance of leadership. In these moments, character is tested and demonstrated. By applying biblical principles consistently, leaders transform tension into trust and difficulty into development—strengthening both relationships and mission.

THE METAPHOR OF A GARDENER PROVIDES A POWERFUL framework for understanding this leadership model. Unlike a dictator who demands uniformity and control, a gardener cultivates conditions for growth. They prepare, nurture, protect, and trust the process of development. They do not force growth—they facilitate it.

In the same way, a servant-hearted leader creates environments where people can thrive. They recognize individuality, invest in development, and exercise patience, understanding that meaningful growth requires time and care. Rather than imposing rigid control, they cultivate potential—allowing individuals and teams to develop according to their design and capacity. When individuals understand their roles, responsibilities, and how decisions are made, many points of friction are naturally eliminated.

Regular team meetings where concerns can be aired, transparent performance review processes, and clear organizational policies all contribute to a more predictable and less conflict-prone environment. Additionally, investing in the development of interpersonal and communication skills for all employees can equip them to handle disagreements more constructively before they escalate.

Like a gardener who plants for future harvests, Kingdom leaders prioritize long-term health over short-term gain. They invest in people, build cultures of trust, and establish systems that sustain growth. Their vision extends beyond immediate outcomes to enduring impact.

This proactive, foresight-driven approach, rooted in creating a well-ordered and communicative environment, aligns with the principle of loving your neighbor by minimizing unnecessary friction and maximizing the potential for harmonious collaboration. It acknowledges that the best way to manage conflict is often to prevent it through thoughtful design and consistent practice.

They also remove obstacles. Whether addressing inefficiencies, providing resources, or eliminating barriers, servant leaders clear pathways for others to succeed. This is not control—it is stewardship.

At its core, this model is relational and interconnected. Just as a garden thrives through balance and mutual support, organizations flourish when collaboration, trust, and shared purpose are cultivated. Leaders foster environments where individuals understand both their value and their contribution to the greater mission.

Trust is central to this process. Having prepared the environment and equipped the team, the leader must trust others to execute. This trust empowers ownership, fuels innovation, and frees leadership to focus on vision and development rather than control.

The greatest work of a gardener is often unseen—and so it is with servant leadership. The quiet investment in people, culture, and systems produces visible fruit over time. True leaders are not driven by recognition, but by the success and growth of those they serve.

This reflects the heart of stewardship. Leaders are entrusted with people, resources, and purpose. Their responsibility is not merely to manage, but to cultivate—to ensure that what has been entrusted to them grows, strengthens, and multiplies.

For this reason, a service-oriented culture must begin at the highest level. It must be modeled, practiced, and consistently demonstrated. When leaders embody servant-heartedness, it permeates the entire organization, creating a culture defined not just by outcomes, but by how those outcomes are achieved.

This requires intentionality. Leaders must continually examine themselves, aligning their actions with the principles they espouse. They must communicate purpose clearly, invest in people consistently, and structure systems that reflect trust, empowerment, and care.

Through accountability, transparency, and humility, leaders create environments where psychological safety thrives and innovation emerges. Individuals who feel valued, supported, and trusted engage more deeply, contribute more fully, and consistently grow.

Over time, this produces a powerful ripple effect. Service becomes not a directive, but a shared culture. Individuals begin to embody these values in their interactions with one another, with clients, and within the broader community.

By consistently applying biblical principles of empathy, truth, reconciliation, and humility, leaders can transform potential crises into opportunities for growth, deeper trust, and a more profound embodiment of Kingdom values within their organizations. This approach not only strengthens the enterprise but also serves as a powerful testimony to the transformative power of Christ-centered leadership in the marketplace and beyond.

This is how a Kingdom enterprise is distinguished—not merely by its success, but by its nature. It is an enterprise where:

- Leadership reflects Christ.
- Authority is expressed through service.
- Power is revealed through humility.

Success is measured not only by outcomes, but by the transformation and the fruitful lives of those it impacts.

NINE
RADICAL INTEGRITY
THE UNSHAKEABLE FOUNDATION

Integrity, within a Kingdom-aligned enterprise, is not an optical virtue or strategic enhancement—it is a foundational mandate rooted in the very character of God. It is the standard by which all actions, decisions, and practices are measured. Without it, any claim to operating under Kingdom principles rings hollow, regardless of outward success or stated values.

Scripture consistently reveals God as the embodiment of truth, justice, and faithfulness. As such, those who represent Him—whether individually or corporately—are called to reflect these attributes in every sphere of life, including business. This is a command, woven throughout the Law, the Prophets, and the demonstrated teachings of Jesus and His apostles.

The Mosaic Law established the foundational pillars of integrity, truthfulness, and fairness for the governance of the Israelite society.

> You shall not steal, you shall not deal falsely, you shall not lie to one another.
>
> LEVITICUS 19:11

This command extends beyond lying as a factual inaccuracy to include any form of deception that misleads, harms, or exploits. In the marketplace, this principle was expressed through the requirement of honest weights and measures:

> You shall not have in your bag two kinds of weights, a large and a small. You shall not have in your house two kinds of ephah, a large and a small. You shall have a full and just weight; you shall have a full and just measure, that your days may be long in the land that the Lord your God is giving you.
>
> DEUTERONOMY 25:13-15

These were not mere economic guidelines or minor ethical preferences. They were a matter of their covenantal alignment with the just and righteous God. The integrity of weights and measures reflected the integrity of their hearts and of the entire economic system. To distort them was to violate both community trust and covenant with God.

The prophets amplified God's integrity standard, often calling out the nation for hypocrisy and corruption. Amos exposed a culture in which leaders overrode righteousness, manipulating systems for personal economic gain at the expense of the vulnerable. He declared:

> Hear this, you who trample on the needy, and make the poor of the land destitute, saying, "When will the New Moon be over, that we may sell our grain? And the Sabbath, that we may offer wheat for sale, making the

> ephah small and the shekel large and dealing deceitfully by false balances, that we may buy the helpless for silver and the needy for a pair of sandals and sell the sweepings of the wheat?"
>
> AMOS 8:4-6

The prophet's judgment upholds integrity as the essential link to God's justice and the protection of the vulnerable. Any business that compromises its integrity participates in a broader system of oppression, regardless of how it is framed. The "false balances" are not just physical tools of deception; they represent a fundamental distortion of fairness and truth in all dealings. The desire to "buy the helpless for silver" speaks to a predatory system that exploits vulnerability—a stark contrast to the spirit of service and the fruitful lives of people that a Kingdom enterprise seeks to cultivate.

In this context, dishonest practices were not isolated infractions—they were symptoms of a deeper moral failure. Integrity, therefore, is inseparable from justice. When profit overrides compassion and justice is distorted, it signals a system that has lost its moral compass—and one that inevitably abandons people.

In the New Testament, integrity is elevated from external compliance to internal transformation. Jesus set the standard with uncompromising clarity, leaving no room for ambiguity or equivocation.

> But let your 'Yes' be 'Yes,' and your 'No,' 'No.' For whatever is more than these is from the evil one.
>
> MATTHEW 5:37 NKJV

His command eliminates ambiguity, manipulation, and performative speech. It establishes a model of radical honesty in which one's word is sufficient because one's character is consistent.

Similarly, every statement, promise, and representation made by the enterprise creates an expectation that it will uphold its words. Any claim about a product or service must be unequivocally true. Anything less constitutes an endorsement of the "evil" that seeks to obscure truth and manipulate others.

Our diligence, our honesty, and our commitment to excellence are to be performed as unto the Lord. The apostle Paul emphasizes the necessity of integrity in Christian conduct within the context of work and commerce—anchoring it in accountability to God.

> Whatever you do, work heartily, as for the Lord and not for men.
>
> COLOSSIANS 3:23 ESV

This perspective reframes all work as an act of obedient worship, compelling us to be people of integrity not because we are being watched, but because our ultimate Audience is the all-seeing God. This also implies that if we are being dishonest or compromising on quality, we are failing to honor God in our work. The integrity of our output, processes, and intentions are all brought under divine scrutiny.

Paul also emphasizes the relational necessity of truth.

> Therefore, having put away falsehood, let each one of you speak the truth with his neighbor, for we are members one of another.
>
> EPHESIANS 4:25 ESV

Truth is not merely an individual virtue; it is the glue that holds communities together. In an organizational setting, this translates to fostering an environment where open, honest communication is normalized. Every communication, action, and form of engagement must be anchored in honesty. Transparency about challenges, honest feedback, and genuine representation of capabilities and limitations are essential principles for building trust with stakeholders. A business that operates with these principles cultivates deep, enduring trust with employees, customers, suppliers, and investors. This trust is not accidental—it is the direct result of consistent, unwavering integrity.

Integrity extends beyond personal conduct to financial dealings as well, a significant aspect of business ethics. The Bible unequivocally emphasizes the importance of financial honesty, while Proverbs abound with warnings against acquiring wealth through deceitful means.

> A false balance is an abomination to the Lord, but a just weight is his delight.
>
> PROVERBS 11:1 ESV

This declaration reveals God's perspective regarding integrity —not as an option, but as His standard. It also establishes a clear contrast: deception is not merely unwise; it is detestable. All accounting practices, pricing strategies, and financial reporting must be scrupulously accurate and transparent. There is no room for creative accounting that obscures reality, no justification for inflating figures, and no defense for hiding losses or liabilities. The goal is not to present a more favorable picture than reality allows, but to represent financial situations truthfully—even when that truth is difficult.

Jesus' teachings emphasize generosity and detachment from greed. The parable of the talents (Matthew 25:14-30) highlights stewardship and accountability for entrusted resources. A dishonest steward will be held accountable. In business, this means managing financial resources with integrity, making sound decisions, and operating with honesty. It includes responsible borrowing, accurate reporting, fair profit distribution, and prudent resource management.

Integrity involves consistency between what is professed and what is practiced. A business that claims values such as customer focus or ethical sourcing but fails to embody them operates without integrity. This hypocrisy erodes trust and undermines its mission. The book of James confronts this misalignment:

> What good is it, my brothers, if someone claims to have faith but has no deeds? Can this faith save him? ... faith by itself, if it does not have works (is not accompanied by action), is dead.
>
> JAMES 2:14, 17 NET (PARAPHRASED)

Applied to enterprise, this principle of faith and works exposes the emptiness of professed values that are not practiced. Regardless of its stated mission or values, a business that lacks honest practices, truthful marketing, and fair treatment of employees ultimately lacks genuine works of integrity.

The implications of this commitment are far-reaching. It requires clear ethical guidelines that are not merely platitudes but actively practiced and modeled by leadership. It demands robust systems of accountability, where deviations are addressed promptly and justly. It necessitates a culture that protects those who speak truth—even when it is uncomfortable—and encourages continual growth in ethical practice.

In a Kingdom enterprise, integrity is the outward manifestation of an inward transformation, a reflection of God's own character in the marketplace. Without this unshakeable foundation, any enterprise seeking alignment with Kingdom principles will ultimately fail, built on shifting sand rather than solid rock. Integrity is the discipline that ensures an enterprise is not merely successful by worldly standards, but righteous and true in the sight of its Creator.

THE BEDROCK OF INTEGRITY IN A KINGDOM-ALIGNED enterprise, as previously established, is a profound commitment to truthfulness, mirroring the very character of God. This unwavering adherence to what is right and true must extend beyond a general disposition to permeate the granular, day-to-day operations of any business. It is in the realm of contracts and communications that this commitment is most rigorously tested and most visibly demonstrated. These are not merely administrative functions; they are the primary vehicles through which an enterprise engages with the world, and thus, they are the most critical arenas for exercising radical integrity.

When we speak of contracts, we are referring to the formal agreements that underpin business transactions. These documents, whether meticulously drafted legal instruments or simpler understandings, represent a solemn promise between parties. For a Kingdom enterprise, the essence of a contract transcends legal enforceability; it embodies a covenant of trust. This implies that every clause, term, and condition must be articulated with utmost clarity and candor, expressed through unvarnished truth. There is no room for ambiguity that could later be exploited, no hidden clauses designed to disadvantage the other party, and certainly no misrepresentation of what is being agreed upon.

Consider the simple act of drawing up an agreement for services. If a company promises a certain deliverable, the contract must accurately reflect that promise. This involves a truthful portrayal of the company's capabilities, the resources it can allocate, and the timeline for completion. It means not over-promising what can be delivered or understating the complexities involved.

For instance, a software development firm should not guarantee a feature that is technically infeasible within the specified timeframe, nor should it fail to disclose potential integration challenges with existing systems. Doing so, even if it secures an immediate contract, sows the seeds of future conflict and damages the enterprise's reputation for honesty. The long-term cost of such deception far outweighs any short-term gain.

True integrity in contracting means acknowledging limitations and uncertainties upfront, allowing the other party to make an informed decision based on reality. This approach builds a foundation of mutual respect and trust, making future collaborations smoother and more productive.

The same standard of unwavering truthfulness must apply to communications, both internal and external. Internal communications are the lifeblood of an organization. When leaders or colleagues communicate with one another, the information shared must be accurate and presented without manipulation. This means being honest about challenges facing the company, the progress of projects, and the performance of individuals.

Transparency, within appropriate boundaries, fosters a sense of shared ownership and encourages problem-solving. Conversely, a culture of withholding information or sugarcoating bad news erodes trust and can lead to significant errors in judgment. Employees who are kept in the dark or fed a steady diet of positive spin are less likely to identify and address critical issues, ultimately harming the enterprise.

Externally, communications encompass everything from marketing and sales pitches to customer service interactions and public relations. The temptation to exaggerate a product's benefits, downplay its drawbacks, or make unsubstantiated claims is often strong in competitive markets. However, a Kingdom enterprise must resist this temptation.

Marketing materials should reflect the genuine value and features of a product or service, not create an illusion of superiority. Sales representatives must be trained to be forthright, providing accurate information about pricing, terms, and product performance. If a product has known limitations or requires specific conditions for optimal use, this information should be readily available. Misleading advertisements or deceptive sales tactics, while they might bring immediate sales, invariably lead to customer dissatisfaction, returns, and a tarnished brand image.

Think of a company selling organic food products. Its marketing might highlight the health benefits and sustainable sourcing. For this to be a practice of integrity, the company must ensure that its products are indeed organic, that their sourcing is genuinely sustainable, and that the claimed health benefits are supported by credible evidence. Any claim of "all-natural" must be scrupulously scrutinized, as definitions can vary and loopholes can be exploited.

If the company uses pesticides under certain conditions or sources from suppliers with less-than-ideal labor practices, these realities must be honestly disclosed, or the marketing claims must be adjusted to accurately reflect the situation. The pursuit of a "halo effect" through misleading branding violates the principle of truth. Instead, the enterprise should focus on communicating the actual, positive attributes of its offerings, building a loyal customer base that values its authenticity.

The consequences of a lack of honesty in contracts and communications are often immediate and devastating. A single instance of deceptive practice can unravel years of trust-building. Imagine a scenario where a supplier provides faulty materials, leading to a product recall or safety incident. If the contract for those materials was poorly drafted, or if the supplier's communications leading up to the agreement were misleading, the damage extends far beyond the cost of the recall. The company's reputation for reliability and quality is undermined. Customers may abandon the brand, suppliers may become hesitant to partner, and investors may lose confidence. Rebuilding this trust is a monumental—often impossible—task.

Conversely, the long-term benefits of unwavering honesty are profound, even transformative. Enterprises that consistently operate with integrity in their contracts and communications build a reputation that becomes one of their most valuable assets. Customers willingly pay a premium for products and services from companies they trust. Employees are more engaged and motivated when they believe in the integrity of their organization. Suppliers are more likely to offer favorable terms and prioritize partnerships with businesses known for fairness and reliability.

Consider a company that has established a reputation for transparent and ethical business practices. When entering into a new contract, the process is often expedited because the other party trusts the company's intentions. Negotiations focus on mutual benefit rather than defensive posturing. Similarly, the company's communications are met with an assumption of truthfulness. Customers are more forgiving of minor issues because they believe the company will address them honestly and fairly. This accumulated goodwill creates a resilient enterprise capable of weathering economic downturns and competitive pressures.

Furthermore, a culture of honesty fosters a positive and productive work environment. When employees feel valued and treated fairly, they are more likely to remain loyal and committed. Open communication channels that encourage feedback and discourage punishment promote better decision-making and innovation. An environment of integrity empowers employees to speak up without fear of repercussions when they identify potential flaws in a product or weaknesses in a proposed strategy.

A candid feedback loop is crucial for course correction and continuous improvement. It prevents minor issues from escalating into major problems, a direct consequence of honesty in all interactions.

> Therefore, having put away falsehood, let each one of you speak the truth with his neighbor, for we are members one of another.
>
> EPHESIANS 4:25 ESV

The Apostle Paul's instruction is particularly relevant in this context. This is not merely about individual moral rectitude—it is communal. In a business context, every communication and every contractual term contributes to the health of the organization and its relationships. Deceit functions like a corrosive agent within the system, while truth is the vital nutrient that sustains and strengthens the enterprise and its stakeholders.

To establish radical integrity in contracts and communications, an enterprise must cultivate deliberate practices. This begins with developing clear ethical guidelines for all forms of communication and contract negotiation. These guidelines should not be abstract principles but actionable directives that precisely define truthful representation and deceptive practices. Secondly, leadership must consistently model these behaviors. If leaders are perceived as less than fully transparent or willing to compromise the truth for convenience, the entire organization will follow suit.

Integrity begins at the top and cascades down. Thirdly, robust systems for accountability are crucial. This involves having mechanisms in place to review contracts for fairness and accuracy, and to monitor marketing and sales practices to ensure they adhere to ethical standards.

Finally, a culture must be established where individuals are empowered to speak truth—even when it is uncomfortable. This includes establishing channels for reporting ethical concerns and protecting whistleblowers from retaliation.

The ongoing commitment to honesty in contracts and communications is not static—it is a continual discipline. There will be moments of pressure to compromise, when a little "white lie" seems harmless, or when a slightly misleading statement could secure a crucial deal. In those moments, integrity, rooted in the character of God, must remain the guiding force. The outcome is not merely a successful business, but one that honors God, builds enduring trust, and demonstrates the power of radical integrity within the broader community—a testament to the goodness of His Kingdom.

WE'VE ESTABLISHED THAT THE FOUNDATION OF INTEGRITY IN A Kingdom-aligned enterprise is a deep commitment to truthfulness, reflecting the very nature of God. For a business aligned with Kingdom values, finances are not merely numbers on a ledger; they are a sacred trust—a reflection of how faithfully the enterprise manages what has been entrusted to it. While truthfulness in contracts and communications is crucial, the financial foundations of an organization demand not just the presence, but the brilliance of exceptional integrity.

Financial stewardship and transparency are not merely administrative functions, they are the primary vehicles through which an enterprise engages with the world. In this realm, they are the most critical arenas for exercising honest performance reporting and ethical accounting principles.

Consider the biblical parable of the talents, where the master entrusted his servants with varying amounts of money. Those who invested wisely and accounted for their gains were rewarded, while the one who buried his talent out of fear, and thus failed to manage it responsibly, faced condemnation.

In a modern enterprise, this means having robust systems in place to track income, expenses, assets, and liabilities. Every invoice received, every payment made, every sale recorded—these are the building blocks of financial truth. Without this granular level of detail, it becomes impossible to truly understand the financial health of the organization, let alone report it accurately to others.

This meticulous record-keeping naturally leads to truthful financial reporting, where an enterprise's commitment to honesty is put under the most intense scrutiny, particularly by external stakeholders such as investors, lenders, and regulatory bodies. Presenting financial statements that are misleading, incomplete, or outright false is not just unethical; it is a violation of trust and, in many jurisdictions, a legal offense. It is akin to bearing false witness.

Kingdom-aligned businesses must ensure that their financial reports—whether quarterly earnings statements, annual reports, or investor presentations—present an accurate and faithful picture of the company's financial position and performance. This means recognizing revenue only when it is earned, expensing costs when they are incurred, and valuing assets at their true worth, not at artificially inflated figures.

Consider the temptation to manipulate earnings. A company might be tempted to recognize revenue prematurely, before all conditions for its earning have been met, simply to meet or exceed analyst expectations. Alternatively, it might delay the recognition of expenses, pushing them into a future period, to make the current period appear more profitable. These are not mere accounting adjustments; they are deliberate acts of deception. The Bible warns against dishonest scales and weights, which were used to defraud customers. In the financial realm, misleading financial statements are the modern equivalent—defrauding investors and creating a false sense of prosperity.

Truth serves as the sole sustainable foundation for growth and trust. True stewardship demands honesty, even when the circumstances are less favorable than desired. It entails presenting the actual state of affairs—whether positive or negative—and trusting that stakeholders will respond to this truth.

Ethical accounting practices are essential to truthful financial reporting. This extends beyond adherence to the letter of the law and requires alignment with the spirit of ethical financial management. It involves avoiding aggressive accounting techniques that obscure reality and establishing strong internal controls to prevent fraud and error. Practices such as segregation of duties and regular internal and external audits are essential in maintaining accuracy and accountability.

Transparency in financial matters stems directly from ethical accounting and truthful reporting. It entails making pertinent financial information accessible to stakeholders in a clear and comprehensible manner. This fosters confidence and trust. Investors are more inclined to allocate resources when they comprehend both risks and opportunities. Employees gain confidence in the organization's stability, resulting in enhanced job security and morale. Customers, particularly in business partnerships where financial stability is a crucial factor, can make informed decisions.

Corporate transparency is not about revealing every proprietary detail that could harm competitive advantage. Rather, it requires clarity about what matters: profitability, debt levels, cash flow, and material risks. For publicly traded companies, this is often mandated by regulations. For privately held businesses, it is a choice that reflects a commitment to integrity. When challenges arise—such as cost overruns or financial strain—transparency means communicating that reality, not burying the losses in footnotes. This commitment to openness reinforces trust and strengthens relationships.

The areas where financial integrity can be compromised are numerous and often subtle. Tax evasion, for example, is not merely a legal issue but a moral one. For Kingdom-aligned businesses, paying taxes is an act of honoring governing authorities (Romans 13:1-7). Deliberately misrepresenting financial income, inflating expenses, or other fraudulent schemes to reduce tax liability is a clear violation of both civic and spiritual responsibility. Essentially, it's stealing from the public good. Similarly, engaging in money laundering or deceptive financial practices directly contradicts the principles of justice and righteousness.

Manipulating financial statements to secure loans or under false pretenses is another serious breach. This could involve overstating assets, understating liabilities, or fabricating revenue streams. Such actions not only deceive stakeholders, but also create a fragile foundation for the business itself. If the business is built on a lie, it cannot sustain long-term success.

> Therefore because you trample on the poor and you exact taxes of grain from him, you have built houses of hewn stone, but you shall not dwell in them; you have planted pleasant vineyards, but you shall not drink their wine.
>
> AMOS 5:11 ESV

The prophet Amos spoke judgment against those who exploited financial systems at the expense of the poor, highlighting the connection between integrity and justice. This principle remains relevant today: financial practices must never be used to exploit vulnerability or advance personal gain at the expense of others.

Financial stewardship includes charitable giving and community investment. While not financial reporting, resource allocation and management reflect the enterprise's integrity. A Kingdom-aligned business should be discerning and ethical in philanthropy, supporting organizations aligned with its values and using funds effectively. Transparency in these efforts builds goodwill and demonstrates a commitment that extends beyond profit.

God cares about how we handle money and possessions. From the parable of the talents to the various instructions in the Mosaic Law regarding fair dealing and the responsible use of wealth, the Bible repeatedly emphasizes accountability and financial responsibility. For a business leader, this clarifies that financial resources are tools to be used for the good of the enterprise, its employees, its customers, and ultimately, for the glory of God.

Ultimately, financial integrity is rooted in stewardship. We are not owners, but managers of what has been entrusted to us, accountable to the highest spiritual authority. Enterprises that uphold financial integrity build enduring trust. Investors are more likely to commit capital, lenders are more inclined to extend credit, employees are motivated to contribute their best efforts, and customers develop loyalty. Over time, this trust becomes one of the organization's most valuable assets.

Conversely, a history of questionable financial practices, even if not outright illegal, can create a persistent cloud of doubt. Rebuilding trust after financial breaches, misleading statements, or a lack of transparency is difficult and often impossible. It requires not only corrected behavior but a genuine transformation of character, demonstrated consistently over time.

Financial stewardship and transparency are not optional—they are integral to the identity of a Kingdom enterprise. They require discipline, accountability, and a steadfast commitment to truth. When upheld, especially when faced with the temptation for expediency or short-term gain, is a profound act of faith and a powerful testament to the enterprise's dedication to managing God's resources with honor and integrity. They safeguard the organization, strengthen its credibility, and contribute to a more just and trustworthy marketplace.

THE PREVIOUS SECTIONS HAVE LAID THE GROUNDWORK FOR understanding integrity as the core of any enterprise aspiring to align with Kingdom values. We have explored its foundational role, the necessity of truthfulness, and the critical dimension of financial stewardship. However, the theoretical framework alone is inadequate until we confront the crucible where integrity is truly forged: pressure. It is during intense challenges, when the easy path diverges sharply from the right path, that the true character of leadership is exposed.

This section delves into the reality of such pressures, offering practical wisdom and scriptural insight to fortify leaders against the storms that inevitably buffet even the most well-intentioned ventures.

The modern business environment presents constant pressure—market volatility, competition, technological change, and the demand for growth. In these moments, the temptation to compromise can be strong. Leaders may feel pressured to misrepresent financial conditions, cut ethical corners, or prioritize short-term survival over long-term integrity.

Consider a company facing a severe downturn: plummeting

sales, overflowing inventory, and dangerously tight cash flow. An anxious board demanding answers and fearful employees create immense pressure to achieve short-term gains, even through unethical means. Leaders may misrepresent financial health for a loan, push defective products to clear inventory, or cut corners on safety to reduce costs. These real dilemmas confront leaders daily, where expediency often overpowering the fear of failure.

Scripture provides powerful examples of individuals who remained steadfast under such pressure—unbroken in their commitment to righteousness. As a young man, Daniel was plucked from his homeland and thrust into the opulent, pagan court of Babylon, and found himself in a position of immense influence. He chose not to compromise his convictions, even in a foreign and hostile environment. His willingness to stand firm, however, led to a deeper respect from his Babylonian captors and ultimately paved the way for him to exercise even greater influence, which he then used to serve God's purposes within the empire. Daniel's story underscores a crucial principle: integrity is built not only in moments of crisis but in the consistent, seemingly minor choices made each day.

Joseph, the son of Jacob, was sold into slavery by his own brothers. He endured immense betrayal and injustice. Despite these hardships, Joseph's diligence and integrity eventually led to his rise as a trusted overseer. When the wife of his master, Potiphar, attempted to seduce him, Joseph refused the temptation not out of fear of Potiphar's earthly authority, although that was a factor, but on a higher moral principle.

> How then can I do this great evil and sin against God?
>
> GENESIS 39:9

Joseph chose God's law despite unjust imprisonment. His integrity, tested by temptation and false accusation, remained unwavering. This unshakeable character distinguished him, leading to his rise to power in Egypt and saving his family and others from famine. Integrity is not about avoiding pressure, but about an internal compass that remains true despite dire circumstances.

In business, these pressures manifest in subtle temptations—embellishing a sales pitch, omitting critical details, accepting a gift that might sway a business decision, even if it's not explicitly a bribe, or making decisions that prioritize convenience over truth. These are the "Potiphar's wife" moments of the business realm, often involving personal relationships, perceived social obligations, or the allure of quick success. In these moments, the question leaders must ask is not, "Can I get away with this?" but "Is this aligned with truth?" The answer to the latter question, guided by a steadfast moral compass, is the hallmark of radical integrity.

Competitive pressures can also tempt leaders toward unethical behavior—misrepresenting competitors, engaging in unfair practices, engaging in industrial espionage, or compromising standards to gain advantage. Imagine a company that has invested heavily in research and development, only to see a competitor quickly replicate their innovation, possibly through illicit means.

The pressure to retaliate in kind, to level the playing field through equally dubious methods, can be immense. However, Kingdom leadership rejects these approaches, choosing instead to compete with excellence, integrity, and trust.

The biblical account of David and Saul is a powerful and complex illustration of competitive pressure and integrity. Saul, consumed by jealousy and insecurity, relentlessly pursued David, seeking to kill him. David had multiple opportunities to take Saul's life, effectively eliminating his competitor and rival for leadership. Yet, David refused. Twice he spared Saul's life, recognizing Saul as God's anointed king, despite Saul's malicious intent.

> The Lord forbid that I should stretch out my hand against the Lord's anointed.
>
> 1 SAMUEL 24:16 KJV (PARAPHRASED)

David's restraint was not born of weakness but of a profound understanding of divine authority and order. This required immense faith and a deep-seated integrity that transcended the immediate political and military realities. Rather than resorting to Machiavellian tactics, he trusted that God would vindicate him and establish him in leadership in His own time and in His own way.

For business leaders, this means resisting the urge to engage in cutthroat tactics, to slander competitors, or to exploit their weaknesses through dishonest means. Instead, the focus should be on building a superior product or service, cultivating strong customer relationships, and competing on the merits of one's own offerings, trusting that ethical conduct will ultimately lead to sustainable success.

The parable of the shrewd manager (Luke 16:1-13) is provocative. Jesus commends the manager's shrewdness in looking after his future, even if his methods were dishonest. However, the context is not to endorse dishonesty but to highlight the contrast between the worldly and spiritual pursuits. It serves as a cautionary tale: if the unrighteous are driven in their pursuits, how much more should those who follow God be driven in their stewardship and integrity? The danger lies in the unrighteous manager's focus on personal gain at the expense of others.

A contemporary example is a CEO orchestrating complex stock options and bonuses exceeding industry norms while the company struggles to maintain profitability. Alternatively, a business owner uses company funds for lavish personal expenses, disguising them as legitimate business expenditures. These actions betray the trust placed in them by shareholders, employees, and stakeholders. The integrity of the enterprise is directly linked to its leadership. When leaders prioritize personal gain over the organization's well-being, they compromise their integrity and sow the seeds of the enterprise's downfall.

> For the love of money is a root of all kinds of evils. It is through this craving that some have wandered away from the faith and pierced themselves with many pangs.
>
> 1 TIMOTHY 6:10 ESV

The apostle Paul advises Timothy that the love of money can manifest as avarice or a relentless pursuit of wealth that disregards ethics.

Navigating these pressures demands intentional discipline. Leaders must cultivate self-awareness of their values and convictions, seek guidance, and remain grounded in their faith. Clear ethical guidelines, accountability systems, and a culture that promotes truthfulness serve as essential safeguards. The practice of "ethical budgeting" – allocating time and resources to ethical training, compliance, and fostering a culture of ethical awareness – is as crucial as financial budgeting.

Developing clear, transparent policies and procedures is crucial. These should address common ethical pitfalls, such as conflict of interest guidelines and whistleblower protection. When employees know expectations and can report concerns without fear of retaliation, ethical breaches are reduced. This creates a systemic defense against pressure, embedding integrity in the organizational culture.

Leadership example is critical. If a leader is willing to make difficult decisions that uphold ethical principles, even when it means sacrificing short-term gain or facing unpopularity, they send a powerful message. When leaders consistently choose integrity—especially when it is costly—they establish a standard that permeates the entire organization. Integrity, when modeled, becomes culture.

Nehemiah's confrontation of the economic exploitation of the poor by the nobles and officials (Nehemiah 5) is a powerful example. Nehemiah did not just issue a decree; he confronted the wrongdoers directly, shamed them, and compelled them to return what they had unjustly taken. His righteous anger and decisive action restored confidence and justice within the community. This willingness to confront wrongdoing, even at the highest levels, is a critical aspect of leading with integrity under pressure.

The enduring value of integrity is the true currency of any enterprise—found in the legacy it creates. This transcends the fluctuations of the market and the ephemeral nature of trends. True leaders understand that integrity is not a mere adherence to rules—it is a disposition of the heart that shapes every decision and interaction. It is the foundation upon which trust is built, loyalty is cultivated, and meaningful impact is achieved.

In the grand tapestry of biblical narrative, we see time and again how individuals and nations that prioritized faithfulness, justice, and truth, even in the face of overwhelming opposition, were ultimately strengthened and blessed. Conversely, those who succumbed to deceit, avarice, and expediency often found their foundations crumbling.

There exists a profound dichotomy between constructing an empire upon shifting sands and establishing a steadfast foundation upon solid rock. The former may initially appear impressive, captivating attention with its dazzling facade, but it ultimately becomes susceptible to the slightest tempest. Conversely, the latter, although potentially demanding greater meticulous effort and unwavering dedication, remains resolute through adversity, its strength emanating from its inherent stability.

The narrative of integrity as a legacy begins with a personal commitment at the leadership level. This translates to a strategic imperative to perceive integrity not as a restrictive factor on profitability, but as a potent catalyst for sustainable growth and positive influence. It is a journey that starts with an inward resolution to align one's actions with deeply held principles.

When leaders consistently choose the harder, right path over the easier, wrong one, they imbue the entire organization with that same ethos. This commitment then becomes the fertile ground from which a culture of integrity can blossom. This culture is not merely a set of policies, but a shared understanding, an unspoken expectation that guides behavior even when formal rules are absent or ambiguous. It is the collective conscience of the organization, shaped by the example and expectations of its leaders.

Beyond internal benefits, integrity reframes work itself. The apostle Paul frequently emphasized the importance of ethical conduct in all spheres of life, including business. His admonition provides a powerful theological underpinning for this concept. As Scripture teaches, all work is ultimately done unto the Lord. This perspective elevates business beyond profit—it becomes a platform to honor God and serve others.

> Whatever you do, work heartily, as for the Lord and not for men, knowing that from the Lord you will receive the inheritance as your reward. You are serving the Lord Christ.
>
> COLOSSIANS 3:23-24 ESV

When this perspective is embraced, the pursuit of integrity becomes an integral part of one's spiritual discipline, transforming the workplace into a sacred space where ethical choices are not just good business, but acts of devotion. When an organization operates with truthfulness, fairness, and compassion, it becomes a living testament to divine principles, a tangible embodiment of Kingdom values in the secular world. This devotional aspect of integrity is crucial in understanding its enduring value. It is not about accumulating accolades or building a personal empire, but about reflecting the character of God in the marketplace.

A legacy of integrity extends beyond financial success. It is measured in lives impacted, communities strengthened, and values upheld. It reflects a commitment to stewardship, responsibility, and purpose, and it requires deliberate action. It involves embedding ethical principles into every aspect of the organization, fostering accountability, and maintaining the courage to uphold truth in all circumstances.

The biblical narrative of Solomon's Temple serves as a compelling example of constructing a legacy of enduring value. While Solomon's later life of compromise serves as a cautionary tale, the Temple itself, built with immense wealth, meticulous craftsmanship, and a profound dedication to God, represented a monumental undertaking designed for perpetuity. It was intended to be a place of worship and a symbol of divine presence that would endure for centuries. This aspiration for permanence, for something that would outlast the builders and serve a higher purpose, is a powerful metaphor for building an organizational legacy. It demands foresight, sacrifice, and an unwavering commitment to principles that transcend the immediate.

Ultimately, a legacy built on radical integrity is an invitation to honor God in the marketplace. It is a declaration that business can be a force for good, a means by which divine principles are enacted and human flourishing is promoted. A Kingdom enterprise is distinguished not only by what it achieves, but by how it achieves it. Integrity is its foundation, its strength, and its legacy.

The reputation for unwavering integrity is not merely a strategic advantage; it is a sacred trust, a profound responsibility, and the most enduring legacy an enterprise can build.

THIS CHAPTER SERVES TO ESTABLISH INTEGRITY AS THE unwavering foundation of a Kingdom-aligned enterprise. It emphasizes that integrity is not merely a principle to be upheld but a discipline to be lived. This discipline shapes decisions, culture, and leadership.

Ultimately, it affirms that true success is measured not only by outcomes but also by the enduring trust, transformed lives, and lasting legacy that reflect the character and values of God's Kingdom.

TEN

THE ENTREPRENEUR AS A STEWARD

MOBILIZING FOR KINGDOM IMPACT

The journey from a divinely inspired vision to a tangible, Kingdom-focused enterprise demands intentionality, strategic planning, and relentless execution. This is the phase where abstract ideals of faith and ethics are forged into concrete realities—daily operations, employee engagement, and market impact. The entrepreneur, acting as a steward of God's provision, mobilizes resources and influence to fulfill a purpose extending far beyond wealth accumulation. The vision becomes a living, breathing entity that actively contributes to stakeholder flourishing and the advancement of God's purposes.

The entrepreneur must first ensure that the foundational vision is not merely a personal ambition but a God-given mandate. This involves deep prayer, seeking clarity on the "why" behind the venture, and discerning alignment with the broader narrative of redemption and restoration. Once divine direction is established, translate it into actionable strategies.

Articulate core values that are not catchy slogans but deeply ingrained principles guiding every decision—from major strategic shifts to the ordinary daily tasks. These values must reflect the character of God: love, justice, mercy, truth, and faithfulness. They serve as the ethical compass for the organization. Without this clear articulation and integration, even the most noble vision can become distorted under marketplace pressures.

The Quadruple Bottom Line Framework

Moving from vision to execution requires a framework that honors both profitability and purpose. A critical element in this transition is adopting a holistic approach to business impact through the *Quadruple Bottom Line* (QBL). Traditional business metrics focus on financial profit. The *Triple Bottom Line*[a] adds social and environmental impact. The QBL elevates this further by explicitly including a spiritual or Kingdom dimension.

Success is measured not only by financial viability, ethical social engagement, and ecological responsibility, but also by the extent to which the enterprise actively contributes to God's purposes, promotes spiritual human flourishing, and serves as a beacon of Kingdom values. As Paul reminds us, "So whether you eat or drink, or whatever you do, do all to the glory of God" (1 Corinthians 10:31). Business operations are no exception.

Implementing the QBL requires conscious integration into strategic planning:

- Financial strategies aim for profitability and ethical wealth generation that can be reinvested for good.
- Social impact initiatives are woven into the business model, addressing societal needs with innovative solutions reflecting God's compassion.
- Environmental stewardship honors creation as responsible caretakers of God's resources.
- Spiritual dimension creates environments where individuals experience spiritual growth, ethical conduct is paramount, and the mission contributes to divine purpose.

Servant Leadership in Action

The Quadruple Bottom Line naturally flows into how leaders actually lead. If the vision is to advance God's purposes, leadership must prioritize others' needs and well-being. Servant leaders, as advocated by Robert Greenleaf[b] and grounded in Christ's example, focus on empowering and uplifting their teams.

Jesus declared, "Whoever would be great among you must be your servant, and whoever would be first among you must be slave of all" (Mark 10:43-44). This is not theoretical; it demands concrete actions: actively listening, showing empathy, fostering belonging, and developing every individual's potential.

Create robust training and development programs. Ensure fair compensation and benefits. Provide safe, supportive work environments. Actively seek feedback from all organizational levels. Leaders serve the collective mission and enable others to succeed rather than wielding authority. Remember, when employees feel genuinely cared for and empowered, their engagement and commitment naturally increase, multiplying the enterprise's impact potential.

Embedding Radical Integrity

Integrity moves from theory to practice by embedding ethical considerations into every operational aspect. Establish clear ethical guidelines for marketing and sales. Ensure financial transparency. Implement fair labor practices beyond legal minimums. Develop responsible sourcing policies.

An entrepreneur might forgo a lucrative but ethically questionable supplier in favor of one that aligns with Kingdom values, even at a higher cost or greater vetting. This isn't about avoiding scandal—it is about proactively building a business that bears witness to truthfulness and righteousness.

> Whoever walks in integrity walks securely, but he who makes his ways crooked will be found out.
>
> PROVERBS 10:9

This commitment builds trust with customers, partners, and within the organization itself, creating a culture where ethical behavior is the norm.

Building A Strategic Plan

Operationalizing the QBL, servant leadership, and radical integrity requires structure. Begin with a clear vision statement and well-defined mission objectives. Review these regularly through prayerful discernment and market realities, ensuring alignment with overarching Kingdom purpose.

Establish key performance indicators (KPIs) for all four dimensions—financial, social, environmental, and spiritual—not just traditional profit metrics. Examples include employee retention rates, customer satisfaction scores, waste or carbon footprint reduction, and quantifiable contributions to community well-being or spiritual growth initiatives.

Communicating The Vision

Strategic clarity means nothing without effective communication. Clearly and consistently communicate vision, values, and strategic objectives to all stakeholders—employees, investors, customers, and the wider community. Communication should be authentic and transparent, reflecting organizational integrity.

Employees particularly need to understand how their individual roles contribute to the larger mission. This fosters purpose and meaning, transforming their jobs into callings. Regular team meetings, internal newsletters, and transparent QBL metric reporting keep everyone aligned and motivated.

Cultivating Resilience

The entrepreneurial journey brings inevitable challenges, and the transition from vision to action is no exception. Moments of doubt, setbacks, and temptations to compromise will arise. During these times, a strong reliance on faith, coupled with a well-defined action plan becomes essential.

The entrepreneur must cultivate resilience, drawing strength from their understanding of God's sovereignty and faithfulness.

> Have I not commanded you? Be strong and courageous. Do not be frightened, and do not be dismayed, for the Lord your God is with you wherever you go.
>
> JOSHUA 1:9

This resilience is not about being impervious to difficulty but responding with wisdom, perseverance, and continued commitment to Kingdom principles.

Practical Integration

Integrating the spiritual dimension of the QBL requires sensitivity. Create opportunities for employees to engage in spiritual disciplines like prayer or Bible study if desired and appropriate within organizational culture. Ensure products or services contribute positively to customers' spiritual well-being, perhaps by providing resources encouraging ethical reflection or personal growth.

This aspect requires sensitivity and respect for diverse beliefs, while focusing on universal principles—love, compassion, and truth—foundational to many religions and particularly central to the Christian worldview informing this book.

Servant leadership implementation requires ongoing development for leaders themselves. This might involve mentorship, coaching, or leadership training programs emphasizing ethical decision-making and relational skills. Leaders must be willing to be vulnerable, admit mistakes, and continuously learn and grow. This modeling of humility and self-awareness is crucial for building healthy, thriving organizational culture.

Integrating radical integrity into the supply chain demands due diligence: selecting suppliers, auditing their practices, and building strong, trust-based relationships. Establish supplier codes of conduct explicitly addressing ethical labor, environmental sustainability, and fair business practices. While this adds complexity and cost, the long-term benefits of a resilient and ethically sound supply chain and positive reputational impact often outweigh the immediate challenges.

A Case Study: Educational Technology Startup

Imagine an entrepreneur with a vision for a technology startup developing educational software. The underlying vision, informed by faith, is to democratize access to quality education, particularly for underserved communities, thereby contributing to human flourishing and the advancement of God's Kingdom through knowledge and empowerment.

Defining core values is the first step in translating vision into action. Alongside innovation and excellence, values such as integrity, compassion, and stewardship become central:

- Integrity: Accurate, ethical educational content; transparent data privacy policies; honest marketing.
- Compassion: Pricing strategies for low-income schools; scholarship programs; accessibility features for learners with disabilities.
- Stewardship: Responsible use of financial resources; efficient operations; environmental sustainability.

The Quadruple Bottom Line integrates into the business plan. Financial success is pursued to enable the company to scale impact and continue its mission. Social impact is measured by the number of students reached, improvements in learning outcomes in target communities, and the creation of educational opportunities for those who might otherwise be deprived of them. Environmental impact metrics are assessed through data center energy consumption and office waste reduction. The spiritual dimension is fostered by cultivating a workplace culture reflecting Christian values, encouraging employees' personal and spiritual growth, and understanding the mission as a service.

Servant leadership is practiced by the CEO and management team. Instead of demanding loyalty, they earn it by supporting their employees, providing professional development opportunities, and creating an environment where innovative ideas are welcomed and challenges are met collaboratively. For example, when the development team faces a technical hurdle, the leaders don't just impose a solution; they facilitate brainstorming sessions, provide necessary resources, and empower the team to find the best way forward, even if it means deviating from the initial plan. This fosters a sense of ownership and intrinsic motivation.

Radical integrity is demonstrated in multiple ways. The marketing team cannot make exaggerated claims about software effectiveness. The sales team is trained for pricing and licensing transparency, especially when dealing with educational institutions with limited budgets. If a bug is discovered, the company immediately issues a patch and communicates openly with its users about the issue and the resolution. If a potential partnership arises with an organization having questionable ethics, the entrepreneur walks away—even if it means foregoing significant revenue—because value alignment is paramount.

The strategic plan includes specific initiatives tied to these principles. A portion of profits funds a foundation providing educational resources to schools in developing countries. Employee performance reviews assess their embodiment of the core values like collaboration and ethical conduct along with technical contributions. Regular all-hands meetings share impact stories, celebrate ethical wins, and reinforce mission—not just discuss sales figures.

Challenges will inevitably arise. Competitors might offer similar products at lower prices by cutting corners on ethical sourcing or data security. Economic downturns can strain the funding for social impact initiatives. During challenging times, an entrepreneur's faith becomes a source of strength, drawing inspiration from biblical stories of unwavering loyalty in the face of adversity. This faith provides encouragement, reminding them that true success is not solely determined by market performance, but by their faithfulness to God's calling.

The decision to prioritize long-term, Kingdom-aligned impact over short-term financial gains is a hallmark of this implementation phase. It requires courage and the deep conviction that God's purposes are ultimately more rewarding and enduring than any temporary marketplace advantages. Moving from strategic planning to sustained impact requires understanding how to deploy every asset God has entrusted to the enterprise. This entrepreneurial steward is not merely building a business—they are building a testament to faith, a force for good, and a tangible expression of God's love and justice in the world.

Ultimately, this enterprise's success is not solely measured by profits and market share, but also by the lives it transforms, the communities it strengthens, and the Kingdom principles it advances through its operations. This active mobilization is the very essence of stewarding God's gifts for His glory and the betterment of humanity.

Mobilizing Resources For Kingdom Impact

The core of mobilization lies in strategic deployment of business assets—not just financial capital, but also intellectual and human resources driving innovation and execution. Financial resources, understood as God-given trusts, are directed with intentionality. Investment decisions are not solely driven by ROI projections but evaluated through the lens of Kingdom impact.

A company might invest in developing affordable, sustainable housing solutions in an area facing a housing crisis. This venture creates economic value while addressing a fundamental human need, reflecting God's heart for the poor and marginalized.

> Whoever oppresses a poor man insults his Maker, but he who is generous to the needy honors him.
>
> PROVERBS 14:31 ESV

This could involve allocating a percentage of profits to a dedicated impact fund, or structuring a business model that inherently benefits underserved communities—employing individuals from disadvantaged backgrounds or sourcing materials from ethical, fair-trade cooperatives. The goal is integrating benevolent purposes into the enterprise's DNA, not viewing charity as an adjunct.

Human capital is equally crucial. Mobilizing talent goes beyond recruitment and retention; it involves cultivating an environment where individuals thrive holistically. Invest in employee development not just for skill enhancement but also character formation. Training programs can incorporate modules on ethical decision-making, spiritual formation, and servant leadership principles, equipping employees as agents of positive change beyond the workplace.

This transforms the workplace into a training ground for Kingdom service. Create opportunities for meaningful service through company-sponsored volunteer initiatives or paid time off for community work. Foster a culture of collaboration and mutual respect where diverse perspectives are valued and each individual feels empowered to contribute unique gifts. When employees understand their work as contributing to a larger, God-honoring purpose, engagement and productivity often soar, creating a virtuous cycle of impact and growth.

Intellectual capital, encompassing knowledge, creativity, and innovation, is another vital resource to be mobilized. Businesses can leverage their expertise to solve pressing societal problems. A software company might develop an accessible platform connecting refugees with essential services. A consulting firm might offer pro bono strategic planning to non-profit organizations struggling with capacity limitations.

This is not merely corporate social responsibility; it's about applying God-given ingenuity and insight to advance His purposes. Identify needs within the community or global arena and intentionally direct research and development efforts, or employee expertise, toward creating solutions. This proactive approach ensures the business is not just a recipient of God's blessings but an active participant in His redemptive work to build, heal, and restore.

Influence, though intangible, is a powerful asset requiring intentional mobilization. Business leaders possess platforms and networks that can be leveraged for the greater good. This might involve advocating for ethical policies in industry associations, engaging in public discourse on matters of justice and compassion, or using influence to connect organizations with needed resources.

Use company marketing channels to raise awareness about critical social issues or to promote values that align with Kingdom principles. When a business demonstrates a consistent commitment to ethical practices and a genuine concern for human flourishing, its voice gains credibility and carries significant weight. This influence can foster systemic change, encouraging other entities to adopt more responsible and benevolent practices, extending the Kingdom's reach far beyond the enterprise's immediate operations.

What, for example, can a manufacturing company do beyond producing goods? It can allocate financial resources to ensure profitability while investing in sustainable manufacturing processes that minimize environmental impact, thereby honoring creation. A portion of profits can be directed toward establishing vocational training centers in economically depressed regions, equipping individuals with marketable skills and offering pathways to dignified employment.

It can mobilize human capital through workforce training in craftsmanship and ethical business conduct. Create opportunities for employees to mentor young people entering the workforce or participate in company-funded community development projects. Use intellectual capital to innovate cleaner production methods or design durable, repairable products that reduce waste. Wield influence by setting high standards for ethical labor practices within the supply chain, encouraging suppliers to adopt similar principles, and advocating for fair trade policies within the sector.

This intentional mobilization testifies to effective stewardship. It recognizes that all assets – financial, human, intellectual, and influential – are ultimately gifts from God, entrusted to the entrepreneur for a purpose transcending personal gain. By strategically directing these gifts towards initiatives addressing societal needs, supporting ministry efforts, and promoting spiritual growth, the business becomes a powerful engine for good, demonstrating that worldly success and eternal objectives are not in conflict but deeply intertwined—actively participating in the building of God's Kingdom while creating a lasting legacy of positive impact.

Stewardship doesn't occur in a vacuum. It unfolds in the rough-and-tumble reality of the marketplace, where Kingdom values meet worldly pressures.

Navigating the Modern Marketplace

Navigating the modern marketplace as an entrepreneur driven by Kingdom values presents a unique and often demanding journey. It is a space characterized by intense competition, shifting consumer expectations, rapid technological advancement, and a pervasive secular ethos that can seem at odds with deeply held spiritual convictions.

Yet, it is precisely within this dynamic environment that the potential for profound impact and witness is amplified. The challenge is not to retreat from the marketplace but to engage with it discerningly, armed with principles ensuring business viability while radiating distinctively ethical and redemptive influence. This requires a deliberate strategy for integrating faith-based values into every facet of operations, transforming the business into a living testimony of God's sovereignty and love.

Establishing Unwavering Ethical Conduct

The first crucial step is establishing unwavering commitment to ethical conduct transcending mere legal compliance. In a world where shortcuts seem tempting and profit pursuit often overshadows moral considerations, the Kingdom-aligned entrepreneur must cultivate a reputation for radical integrity.

Every transaction, contract, advertising claim, and customer interaction is viewed through the lens of truthfulness, fairness, and respect. Be scrupulously honest about product capabilities.

Be transparent about pricing. Be unwavering in fulfilling promises. A company committed to Kingdom values would not engage in deceptive marketing practices, even if those practices are common in the industry. Instead, focus on clear, honest communication empowering consumers to make informed decisions.

Likewise, when faced with opportunities to exploit loopholes or engage in practices that, while legal, are morally questionable, the entrepreneur must possess courage and conviction to abstain. This unwavering commitment builds trust—a currency more valuable than any short-term financial gain. Trust fosters customer loyalty, attracts like-minded partners, and creates a stable foundation for long-term success.

Reframing Competition

Competition in the modern marketplace is fierce. Entrepreneurs guided by Kingdom values may sometimes feel at a disadvantage when facing competitors who prioritize profit above all else. However, a Kingdom perspective reframes this challenge.

Instead of viewing competitors solely as rivals to be vanquished, see them as fellow actors in the same economic sphere, albeit with different motivations and operating principles. Adopt a posture of healthy competition, focusing on delivering superior value through innovation, quality, and exceptional service—all underpinned by integrity.

Explore opportunities for collaboration with other businesses, even those with different values, on projects serving a common good or addressing shared industry challenges. This doesn't imply compromising core principles but seeking areas of mutual interest where ethical engagement is possible. A Christian-owned business might collaborate with other companies on industry-wide initiatives to improve environmental sustainability or develop training programs elevating workforce skills across the sector. Such collaborations, rooted in shared objectives rather than ideological alignment, can foster positive industry-wide change and demonstrate how ethical business practices can be both principled and pragmatic.

Influencing Culture Through Business

Businesses are not merely economic entities; they are social actors that shape perceptions, set standards, and influence behavior. An entrepreneur operating with Kingdom values has a unique opportunity to imbue their enterprise with principles that can counteract negative cultural trends.

Create a workplace culture that prioritizes employee well-being, dignity, and mutual respect, even in high-pressure environments. Champion diversity and inclusion, not just as social justice but as an expression of God's creation, where every individual, regardless of background, is valued and empowered.

Beyond internal operations, use the business's voice and resources to advocate for policies and practices promoting ethical behavior, social responsibility, and compassion in the wider community. Support charitable organizations, engage in public discourse on critical social issues, or use marketing platforms to highlight stories of hope and positive change. The goal is to be a leavening agent, subtly transforming the societal landscape through consistent, principled action.

Engaging Stakeholders with Kingdom Values

Engaging stakeholders—employees, customers, suppliers, investors, and the community—requires a nuanced approach reflecting Kingdom values. Employees are not simply a cost of doing business but individuals made in God's image, deserving dignity, fair treatment, and growth opportunities. Provide competitive wages and benefits, invest in professional development, foster supportive and safe work environments, and practice transparent communication.

Treat customers with respect and honesty, offering products and services genuinely meeting their needs and delivering on promises. Engage suppliers with fairness and integrity, fostering long-term relationships built on mutual trust. Investors, whether aligned with the Kingdom vision or not, should be treated with transparency regarding the company's performance and its ethical commitments. The community, in turn, benefits from a business that acts as a responsible corporate citizen, contributing positively to its economic and social well-being.

This holistic approach to stakeholder engagement ensures that the business creates value for all involved, reinforcing the idea that Kingdom businesses are designed for fruitful impact, not merely profit.

Maintaining Ethics In A Globalized Marketplace

Competing in a globalized marketplace, characterized by diverse legal and ethical standards, further tests the resolve of the Kingdom-aligned entrepreneur. Navigating international supply chains requires diligence to ensure labor practices and environmental standards align with Kingdom principles, even in regions where such standards may be lax.

Invest in rigorous supplier auditing, choose to forgo partnerships with entities engaging in exploitative practices, and actively seek suppliers who demonstrate commitment to ethical conduct. Marketing campaigns directed at international audiences must be culturally sensitive and ethically sound, avoiding manipulation or misrepresentation.

This commitment to ethical consistency across all markets, regardless of local norms, is a powerful differentiator and testament to unwavering adherence to Kingdom values. It demonstrates that the business's moral compass is not subject to geographical boundaries or market pressures.

The entrepreneur must be prepared to articulate the unique value proposition of a Kingdom-aligned business. This is not merely about selling a product or service, but offering a distinct experience rooted in trustworthiness, ethical service, and a higher purpose. Customers and partners are increasingly seeking businesses aligning with their own values.

Transparency and authenticity build brand loyalty and differentiate the business in a crowded marketplace. A company genuinely demonstrating commitment to integrity, social responsibility, and positive impact can attract a loyal following. This requires clear communication about the company's mission, values, and tangible ways it seeks to make a positive difference. Storytelling becomes a powerful tool, sharing narratives of how the business has positively impacted employees, customers, or communities while maintaining commitment to ethical principles.

Innovation Within a Kingdom Framework

Innovation within a Kingdom framework takes on a unique dimension. Innovation should not be solely driven by desire for market dominance or increased efficiency at any cost. Instead, it should be guided by a desire to solve problems, meet needs, and enhance human flourishing in ways aligning with Kingdom principles.

Develop products that are more sustainable, accessible, or beneficial to society. Find innovative ways to improve employee well-being or engage the community meaningfully. The entrepreneurial spirit, coupled with a Kingdom ethos, can lead to groundbreaking solutions that are both economically viable and ethically sound.

A tech company might focus innovation efforts on developing assistive technologies for individuals with disabilities. A food company might innovate around sustainable agriculture practices benefiting both the environment and local farming communities.

Navigating the modern marketplace with Kingdom values is an ongoing act of faith and discernment. It requires deep understanding of biblical principles, courageous commitment to applying them in the complexities of commercial life, and willingness to learn and adapt.

The entrepreneur is called to be a faithful steward, using their business as a platform to demonstrate God's goodness, justice, and love. This is not about creating a "Christian business" in isolation but operating a business in a distinctly Christian way —with integrity, compassion, and commitment to making a positive, redemptive impact on the world. Consistent embodiment of these principles not only builds a successful enterprise but also contributes to the advancement of God's Kingdom, transforming the marketplace one principled decision at a time.

The integration of faith into the fabric of enterprise is not a passive endorsement, but an active, dynamic engagement with the world, offering a compelling alternative to purely secular approaches to commerce and proving that ethical considerations are not a barrier to success, but rather a pathway to deeper, more meaningful achievement and lasting influence.

Redefining Success

The entrepreneur's role extends to challenging prevailing norms and redefining success. In a culture fixated on metrics like sales volume, market share, or rapid financial growth, a Kingdom-aligned business introduces a broader definition of prosperity encompassing financial sustainability, the well-being of people and planet, and contribution to a just and flourishing society.

This redefinition requires conscious effort to communicate and demonstrate that ethical practices, fair labor, environmental stewardship, and community engagement are not optional add-ons but integral components of truly successful enterprise. When a business consistently prioritizes these aspects, it begins shifting perceptions within its industry and among consumers, fostering a ripple effect encouraging greater ethical awareness and responsibility.

The entrepreneur as a steward must cultivate resilience in the face of adversity, which is inevitable in the business world. Market downturns, unexpected competition, regulatory changes, and internal challenges can all test resolve. However, a foundation in Kingdom values provides a unique source of strength. This is a long-term endeavor, requiring patience and perseverance, but the impact of such a paradigm shift can be transformative.

Recalling biblical narratives of faithfulness amid trials—the perseverance of early apostles or the unwavering trust of individuals like Joseph, son of Jacob, facing betrayal—offers profound encouragement. This resilience is not about avoiding difficulty but navigating it with wisdom, grace, and unwavering commitment to core principles.

Learn from setbacks, adapt strategies without compromising values, and maintain a long-term perspective that transcends immediate pressures. The ability to weather storms with integrity and faith serves as a powerful testament and inspires confidence among stakeholders.

Strategic Communication

Intentional engagement with the marketplace involves strategic communication. It is insufficient to simply *operate* with integrity; one must also *communicate* that integrity effectively and authentically. Be transparent about the company's values, its mission, and its impact. Marketing materials, website content, annual reports, and public statements should all reflect the core principles that guide the business.

This transparency is a powerful tool for differentiation, attracting customers and partners who resonate with the company's ethical stance. It also educates stakeholders about the possibilities of doing business differently. A company might highlight its commitment to fair trade sourcing by sharing stories about partner farmers and the positive impact of those relationships. This not only builds brand loyalty but also contributes to a broader cultural conversation about responsible consumption and ethical production.

The entrepreneur must be a lifelong learner, continuously seeking to deepen understanding of how to apply Kingdom values in an evolving marketplace. This might involve engaging with theological resources, studying business ethics, participating in peer networks of like-minded entrepreneurs, and remaining open to feedback from employees and customers.

The marketplace is not static, and what worked yesterday may not be sufficient tomorrow. Stay abreast of industry trends, technological advancements, and societal shifts—not to chase fleeting fads but to discern how to navigate changes in ways remaining faithful to enduring principles. This commitment to continuous learning and adaptation ensures the business remains relevant, effective, and a powerful force for good.

In essence, navigating the modern marketplace with Kingdom values is about more than conducting business ethically; it is about actively participating in God's redemptive work within the economic sphere. It demonstrates that business can be a powerful instrument for good, fostering human flourishing, promoting justice, and reflecting God's character.

This endeavor requires courage, creativity, perseverance, and unwavering reliance on divine wisdom. When entrepreneurs embrace this calling, they not only build enduring businesses but also contribute to a more just, compassionate, and sustainable world, proving that Kingdom principles are not only relevant but transformative in the very heart of commerce. The sustained practice of these principles builds a legacy extending far beyond financial success, impacting lives and shaping culture for the better—a tangible manifestation of faith in action.

All of this—the strategic planning, the ethical decision-making, the marketplace engagement—requires one indispensable quality: courage.

The Call To Courageous Stewardship

The entrepreneurial journey inherently demands courage. It is a path fraught with uncertainty, where the entrepreneur willingly steps into the unknown, investing not just capital but also dreams and considerable personal energy into ventures that may or may not materialize. This inherent risk-taking, however, is not merely a characteristic of secular ambition; it finds a profound and deeply spiritual echo in the biblical call to courageous stewardship.

When we consider the lives of biblical figures who operated within their respective economic and social spheres, we find compelling examples of individuals who demonstrated extraordinary courage in the face of daunting odds, all while maintaining deep-seated commitment to a higher calling.

Joseph of Arimathea: A Model of Courageous Action

Let's revisit Joseph of Arimathea. He did not shy away from controversy or potential ostracization; instead, he acted decisively, driven by a conviction that transcended the immediate political and social pressures. His decisive act of stewardship over Jesus' body—preparing it and laying it in his own tomb—was a profound declaration of faith and courageous allegiance.

This same spirit of courageous stewardship is precisely what is required of the modern entrepreneur who seeks to build an enterprise that not only thrives financially but also honors God and contributes to His redemptive purposes. The entrepreneur is called to step out from the perceived safety of the familiar and embrace the challenging path of building something new, something reflecting Kingdom values. This stepping out is not a blind leap of faith but a calculated venture rooted in trust in divine guidance and provision. Just as Joseph trusted that his actions, though fraught with risk, were aligned with a divine narrative, so too must the modern entrepreneur trust that their diligent efforts, undertaken with integrity and a heart for service, are part of God's larger plan.

Innovation As Prophetic Action

The entrepreneurial call to courage is amplified when we consider the very nature of innovation and market disruption. To create something truly new is to challenge the status quo, to venture into territory where established norms are questioned, and where resistance is often encountered. This requires steadfast belief in the vision, resilience to overcome obstacles, and willingness to endure criticism from those invested in maintaining existing paradigms.

This is precisely the arena where Kingdom values can shine most brightly. When an entrepreneur introduces a business model prioritizing ethical practices, fair compensation, or environmental sustainability in an industry notorious for cutting corners, they are not simply making a business decision—they are making a prophetic statement. They are declaring that there is a better way, a way that honors both profitability and principle. For the Kingdom-aligned entrepreneur, courage is infused with a spiritual dimension: the courage to believe that God's design for success can be realized through their business, even when the prevailing economic climate or industry trends suggest otherwise.

Biblical Precedents for Facing Giants

The stories within Scripture are replete with individuals who were called to step out of their comfort zones and embark on seemingly impossible tasks. Moses led the Israelites out of Egypt, facing the most powerful empire of his day. Gideon gathered an unlikely army of three hundred to defeat overwhelming forces. David faced the giant Goliath with nothing but a sling and stones. These are not tales of effortless victory but of individuals who, despite their fears and limitations, chose to obey and act in faith, trusting in God's power to bring about His will.

The modern entrepreneur faces similar, albeit different, kinds of giants—dominant market players, entrenched industry practices, or complex regulatory landscapes. The call to courageous stewardship means refusing to be intimidated by these challenges, choosing instead to forge ahead with a spirit of innovation and dependence on God. We cultivate a mindset that sees obstacles not as insurmountable barriers but as opportunities for divine intervention and creative problem-solving.

The Foundation of Spiritual Resilience

True entrepreneurial courage is sustained by drawing strength from a deep well of spiritual resilience—prayer, Scripture, and community. "Trust in the Lord with all your heart, and do not lean on your own understanding. In all your ways acknowledge him, and he will make straight your paths" (Proverbs 3:5-6). We must understand that true success is not measured solely by financial returns, but by the faithfulness with which one stewards the resources and opportunities entrusted to them.

The notion of stewardship implies responsibility and accountability. Stewards are not owners; they are managers entrusted with resources that belong to another. "Moreover, it is required of stewards that they be found faithful" (1 Corinthians 4:2). As Kingdom entrepreneurs, we steward talent, capital, time, and influence—but ultimately these belong to God. Therefore, the courage to build and to lead is intrinsically linked to the responsibility to manage His resources wisely and ethically, in alignment with His purposes.

This is the hallmark of Kingdom entrepreneurship. It is a courage born not of self-confidence but of confidence in God's sovereignty and faithfulness.

A True Steward's Legacy

Just as Joseph of Arimathea stepped forward at a critical moment, modern entrepreneurs are called to step forward in their own contexts, using their businesses as platforms for demonstrating God's love, justice, and redemptive power. This is not about building religious enterprises separate from the world but about building excellent, competitive, innovative businesses that operate according to Kingdom principles, thereby transforming the marketplace from within.

The transition from divinely inspired vision to Kingdom-focused enterprise is an ongoing process of intentionality and adaptation. It requires the entrepreneur to be not just a visionary but also a strategist, a leader, and a faithful steward, committed to building an organization that reflects God's character and contributes to His purposes in the world.

This active mobilization of resources and influence, guided by unwavering commitment to Kingdom imperatives, is what transforms a business from a mere economic entity into a powerful force for good. When entrepreneurs embrace this calling with courage, strategic thinking, and faithful stewardship, they not only build successful enterprises but also advance God's Kingdom, leaving lasting legacies of positive impact that extend far beyond the bottom line.

FINAL WORDS

If you have journeyed with me through this book, you have already opened your mind to consider God's perspective on how we are to be about our Father's business.

At the beginning of this narrative, I suggested a shift from measuring success by the prosperity of Joseph, son of Jacob, to measuring it by the courageous stewardship of Joseph of Arimathea. Joseph in Egypt teaches us how God can use wisdom, planning, and power to preserve nations. Joseph of Arimathea teaches us something even more radical: that Kingdom wealth finds its highest expression not in what it accumulates, but in what it is willing to risk and release to protect what is most precious to God.

That is the heart of your own Arimathean Assignment.

You have been entrusted with resources, relationships, and opportunities that are not accidental. Your capital, your creativity, your networks, and your authority are all part of a sacred trust. The question is no longer merely, "How much can this business grow?" but "What—whom—am I protecting, preserving, and advancing for the sake of Christ and His Kingdom?"

In Joseph of Arimathea's moment, faithful stewardship meant stepping out of the shadows, identifying with a crucified Messiah, and offering his own tomb at precisely the time it was most costly to do so. For you, it may look like:

- **Choosing** radical integrity when compromise would be more convenient.
- **Structuring** your company so that people are not used up, but genuinely flourish.
- **Ordering** your metrics and strategies around a Quadruple Bottom Line—People, Planet, Profitability, and Eternity.
- **Saying** "no" to opportunities that would erode the spiritual and moral center of your work, even if they promise short-term gain.

You are not merely an owner or an executive. You are a steward. God is the true CEO and ultimate shareholder of your enterprise. Your role is to listen, to align, and to act—turning conviction into policy, prayer into strategy, and worship into daily operational decisions.

If you are part of the Body of Christ, then you are one that carries the power, authority, and presence of the Holy Spirit. He is the source of the wisdom that Joseph, son of Jacob used to build, plan, and lead with excellence—and He is the source of the courage Joseph of Arimathea accessed to step forward when it would be easier to stay hidden.

Your assignment is not just to create wealth, but to safeguard the vulnerable, to underwrite redemptive work, and to protect the witness of Christ within you in the marketplace. Ultimately, that is our greatest takeaway concerning *The Arimathean Assignment.* Now is your moment to steward it.

As you close this book, my prayer is that you will embrace a first-responder mentality in God's Kingdom: that you will see your company as one of the first on the scene when there is need, injustice, or spiritual vulnerability.

And above all, may you hear, one day, the only evaluation that finally matters over your life and enterprise: "Well done, good and faithful servant."

Dr. John Thurber

GLOSSARY

Arimathean Assignment: The unique call and responsibility entrusted by God to an individual to leverage their resources, talents, and influence for the advancement of His Kingdom, particularly within their sphere of influence (e.g., the marketplace). This concept is inspired by Joseph of Arimathea's courageous act of providing a tomb for Jesus.

Biblical Stewardship: The concept of managing resources (time, talent, capital, influence) on behalf of God, recognizing Him as the ultimate owner and seeking to use these resources in ways that honor His will and advance His purposes.

Eschatological Focus: A perspective that views present actions and endeavors through the lens of future, eternal outcomes, prioritizing values and impacts that transcend earthly and temporal concerns.

Generational Impact: The enduring influence of an enterprise or individual's actions and values that extends beyond their own lifetime, shaping subsequent generations.

Kingdom Entrepreneurship: A business philosophy and practice that prioritizes Kingdom values, ethics, and objectives alongside or above traditional profit motives. It involves integrating faith into every aspect of business operations, with the ultimate goal of glorifying God and serving humanity.

Kingdompreneur: An individual with an operative belief, motive, and approach to business that is intentionally oriented toward advancing God's reign and purposes in the world, integrating faith, ethics, and economic activity.

Legacy Building: The intentional process of creating a lasting positive impact and enduring value that continues to bear fruit long after the founder's direct involvement.

Sacred Trust: The understanding that business assets, opportunities, and responsibilities are not merely personal possessions but are entrusted by God to be managed faithfully for His glory.

Servant Leadership: A leadership model that prioritizes the needs of others, focusing on empowering, equipping, and developing individuals within the organization and the broader community.

Spiritual Capital: The intangible assets derived from a deep-rooted faith—such as integrity, trust, wisdom, and a strong ethical compass—that shape behavior and foster resilience and long-term success.

Theological Economics: The study and practice of economic principles informed by theological truths, emphasizing justice, compassion, and human flourishing as integral components of economic activity.

NOTES

10. THE ENTREPRENEUR AS A STEWARD

a. John Elkington, *Cannibals with Forks: The Triple Bottom Line of 21st Century Business.* (Oxford: Capstone, 1997).
b. Robert K. Greenleaf, *Servant Leadership: A Journey into the Nature of Legitimate Power and Greatness* (Mahwah, NJ: Paulist Press, 1977).

BIBLIOGRAPHY

Myles, Francis. "The 'Other Joseph' God Showed Me About Kingdom Entrepreneurship w/Taylor Welch." *YouTube video*, 37:13. December 9, 2025. https://youtu.be/XAqid_sT6Sw.

Elkington, John. *Cannibals with Forks: The Triple Bottom Line of 21st Century Business.* Oxford: Capstone, 1997.

Greenleaf, Robert K. *Servant Leadership: A Journey into the Nature of Legitimate Power and Greatness.* Mahwah, NJ: Paulist Press, 1977.

ABOUT THE AUTHOR

Dr. John Thurber is an American minister and author. John ministers in his local congregation in an evangelistic businessman capacity, teaching Kingdom business principles. He also serves as lead visionary using entrepreneurial skills to launch, grow, build and assist business owners in making God's destiny a reality, and funding the Kingdom for the outreach of the gospel.

John holds a Doctor of Religious Education from Destiny Christian University and is the proud Daddy to Colemon, Atlee, and Brynlee. They live in Oklahoma where he puts his entrepreneurial spirit to work in business.

ALSO BY DR. JOHN THURBER

The Father Code: A Biblical Perspctive On Fatherhood

The Father Code: Workbook

www.ingramcontent.com/pod-product-compliance
Lightning Source LLC
LaVergne TN
LVHW010917110826
845149LV00013B/2390

9798991854245